014387897 Liverpool Univ

KU-620-510

SHORT CUTS

INTRODUCTIONS TO FILM STUDIES

WITHDRAWN
FROM STOCK

CONTEMPORARY BRITISH CINEMA

FROM HERITAGE TO HORROR

JAMES LEGGOTT

WALLFLOWER

LONDON and NEW YORK

First published in Great Britain in 2008 by
Wallflower Press
6 Market Place, London W1W 8AF
www.wallflowerpress.co.uk

Copyright © James Leggott 2008

The moral right of James Leggott to be identified as the author of this
work has been asserted in accordance with the Copyright, Designs and
Patents Act of 1988

All rights reserved. No part of this publication may be reproduced,
stored in a retrieval system, or transported in any form or by any means,
electronic, mechanical, photocopying, recording or otherwise, without the
prior permission of both the copyright owner and the above publisher of
this book

A catalogue record for this book is available from the British Library

ISBN 978 1 905674 71 8

Series design by Rob Bowden Design

Printed in the UK by Cromwell Press, Trowbridge, Wiltshire

CONTENTS

ACKNOWLEDGEMENTS

I would like to thank my colleagues at Northumbria University for their support, especially Tobias Hochscherf and Peter Hutchings for their amiable and informative chats about British cinema. I also appreciate the patience and editorial assistance of Yoram Allon, Jacqueline Downs, Ian Cooper and all at Wallflower Press.

I am grateful for the generous support of my family. My deepest thanks go to Karen for her proofing, patience and exposure to some terrible movies.

INTRODUCTION

This book is concerned with British film culture in the years between 1997 and 2008. It offers a survey of filmmaking during this period, and a summary of the major debates around contemporary British cinema. But what exactly *is* British cinema, and how might we distinguish or contextualise its recent manifestations? These questions have prompted intense discussion among academics, journalists and cinemagoers. They are complicated further by the recognition amongst scholars that a national cinema is as problematic to define as a national identity, and that the link between the two is far from straightforward.

Whilst the analysis here seeks to identify the ways in which contemporary British film production might be defined and categorised, it also illustrates the very problems of doing so. The characteristic qualities of British film culture have been greatly contested, to the extent that contemporary British cinema is perhaps most usefully defined as a *debate*, an on-going conversation about quality and purpose. For the scholar wishing to intervene, this is a stimulating but daunting prospect, particularly as the legacy and influence of any present-day cultural phenomenon is, by definition, near impossible to assess.

A further difficulty in drawing conclusions about the contemporary era of British cinema arises from its somewhat convenient definition, for the purposes of this survey, as the years following the election of Tony Blair and a Labour government in 1997. Like nearly all acts of historical periodisation, this is a critical construct, justly open to cross-examination. To imply that the period under scrutiny here marks an utterly discrete, distinct block of history – cinematic or otherwise – would be misguided. The unfolding of history is a dynamic process, and the events that took place in the Blair and Brown years are ultimately the result of currents and tendencies stretching further back in time.

Another country? Prime Minister Blair (Michael Sheen) takes a telephone call from the monarch in *The Queen*

However, a focus upon the cinematic output of the Blair years has some benefits of neatness, not least because this book happened to be completed in the months following the succession of Gordon Brown as Prime Minister in late June 2007. A decade earlier, in May 1997, Tony Blair had brought an end to 18 years of Conservative government with a land-slide electoral victory for his 'modernising' Labour Party. There was little doubt at the time, or ten years later, that this was a significant moment in Britain's political history, even though the New Labour project of shifting the party to the middle of the British political spectrum had been some time in development.

However, as acknowledged implicitly by *The Queen* (2006), the preced-ing decade quickly felt like another country, another world altogether. The events of 11 September 2001, and the related terrorist attacks in subse-quent years in Madrid, London and elsewhere, pushed international rela-tions and domestic security high up the political and cultural agenda. In Stephen Frears' perceptive docu-drama about the aftermath of the death of Princess Diana in August 1997 – a story still appearing in UK headlines ten years later, and also invoked in the promotional material for *The Duchess* (2008), a historical drama based on a best-selling biography of one of her ancestors – a gauche, newly-elected Prime Minister (Michael Sheen) counsels the Royal Family in the art of spin and popular empathy. For contemporary audiences the irony was delicious. Having achieved in

1997 the highest approval levels of any British Prime Minister to date, Blair now commanded the lowest of any Labour leader (see Jones 2006), mostly as the result of his hugely unpopular military campaigns in Afghanistan and Iraq.

In the context of such a serious political climate, it may seem flippant to draw an analogy between the fluctuating popularity of the Prime Minister and the rollercoaster fortunes of the British film industry during his time in office. But the upbeat message of the pop song adopted by the Labour Party for its 1997 election campaign – D: Ream's 'Things Can Only Get Better' – seemed equally applicable to the industry. A successful string of films in the preceding years, including *Four Weddings and a Funeral* (1994), *Trainspotting* (1996), *The English Patient* (1996) and *The Full Monty* (1997), together with the prospect of a sympathetic new government, created a mood of buoyancy. However, within a few years there was palpable disappointment about the quality of some of the films supported by UK Lottery funding, and anxiety about how a market-driven, target-led ideology might be shaping British film culture.

This book seeks to do justice to the diversity of British filmmaking in the Blair era (and beyond) by using a range of films – some better-known than others – to advance and illustrate questions of industry, culture, representation and genre. The structure is as follows: chapter 1 introduces the various ways in which contemporary British cinema might be defined and judged; chapter 2 elaborates upon the key debates around the national cinema through an overview of the most significant aspects of Britain's film industry and culture; chapter 3, on key genres, considers the types of storytelling that have dominated British filmmaking in recent years, including the horror film, the historical film and the romantic comedy; chapter 4 pays attention to important aspects of representation, namely the depiction of class, gender, ethnicity and sexuality.

A book of this length on such an ill-defined subject necessitates a certain selectivity of focus. For reasons of space, films made in Ireland (including Northern Ireland) are not considered. Furthermore, the term 'cinema' is mostly defined as films of feature length that have been released theatrically. Filmmaking activities taking place or being consumed beyond the industrial mainstream are not dwelt upon at length here, but this is not to suggest that work such as video art, short films and features distributed independently or online do not warrant analysis.

The goal of this study is a modest one. British film scholarship is at present a lively and expanding field but, speaking anecdotally, I have found that discussion of contemporary British cinema with students, lecturers and fellow cineastes in the UK is all too often met with resistance, and sometimes even hostility. This exasperation with the national cinema is understandable, but the reluctance to engage critically with it is disheartening. If nothing else, this book attempts to prove why contemporary British filmmaking might be worthy of our attention, if not necessarily our affection.

1   DEFINITIONS AND APPROACHES

Scholars of British cinema are far from alone in their struggle to define, analyse and measure the worth of contemporary filmmaking. Discussion of the quality and purpose of British film culture is not only sport for academics, but for journalists, government policy-makers, audience members and filmmakers themselves. Sometimes their various criteria of evaluation overlap, but often they do not. This is hardly surprising, given the divergent ways of assessing the effectiveness of the national cinema, which include indigenous relevance, creative accomplishment, the promotion of British culture and heritage (including the impact upon the tourist industry), the level of success in international festivals and award ceremonies, the scope it gives for complex and interesting performances, and the generation of revenue domestically and worldwide.

A contemporary snapshot

If the health of a film culture can be measured by way of its visibility, range and budding talent, then British cinema seemed to be in good shape in the early days of Gordon Brown's premiership. In late summer 2007, there was an impressive variety of home-grown product to lure the British moviegoer into his or her local multiplex or independent cinema.

Joe Wright's *Atonement* (2007), an epic visualisation of Ian McEwan's novel, was ideal for those who liked their drama prestigious and literary, with the added bonus of performances by rising young actors, such as James McAvoy and Keira Knightley, with international kudos, and the involvement of Working Title, arguably the UK's most successful production company. The Edinburgh-set *Hallam Foe* (2007) was another literary adaptation, but offered edgier fare, as well as confirmation of the blossoming careers of its director (David Mackenzie) and main star (Jamie Bell). More populist, but no less intriguing a proposition, was *Run, Fat Boy, Run* (2007), which boasted a central performance and script by Simon Pegg, part of the creative team behind the immensely pleasurable *Hot Fuzz* (2006). Throughout September 2007, *Run, Fat Boy, Run* remained top of the UK box office, pushing *Atonement* into second (and for one week third) place in an otherwise Hollywood-dominated chart.[1] There was also still a chance to catch *Harry Potter and the Order of the Phoenix* and, for those quick enough, *Rise of the Footsoldier*, a gangster film aimed squarely at the native audience.

Meanwhile, the high-profile DVD releases of films that had already gained prominence that year – the likes of *Venus* (2006), *This is England* (2006), *Becoming Jane* (2007), *28 Weeks Later* (2007), *Sunshine* (2007) and *Mr Bean's Holiday* (2007) – seemed proof enough that the British film industry was catering to diverse tastes, whilst the appearance of career-spanning box sets of work by Ken Loach and Shane Meadows reflected the esteem held for its social chroniclers. Furthermore, the BBC's heavily promoted Summer of British Film season of documentaries and screenings offered a celebratory survey of the national cinema, contextualising recent successes and fostering anticipation for forthcoming attractions such as *Sleuth* (2007), *Elizabeth: The Golden Age* (2007) and *St Trinian's* (2007).

Despite the apparent buoyancy of the industry in 2007 – an impression bolstered in part by the Academy Award victories for *The Queen* and *The Last King of Scotland* (2006) – the year's releases provoked some all too familiar questions. Indeed, every optimistic sign stood the risk of negation by recurring anxieties about the direction of British cinema. If the tendency towards high-profile sequels and remakes was emblematic of a reflective turn in the wider culture, offering a space for some kind of interrogation of Britishness past and present, it also spoke of a lazy attempt to revive former glories.

With its budget of £20 million, unusually high for a UK production, *Atonement* had the clout to compete directly with Hollywood, but its evocation of a 'quality' tradition of exportable costume drama caused disquiet in some quarters. In his review for *The Sunday Times*, Cosmo Landesman called to mind academic debates around so-called 'heritage' cinema (see chapter 3) by noting how the film 'ooz[ed] good taste, cultural refinement and what people call classiness' but was, in fact, merely a 'snobbish, middlebrow drama' (2007: 10). Although *The Queen* could be praised – together with other contemporaneous docu-dramas like *United 93* (2006), *The Road to Guantánamo* (2006) and *Ghosts* (2006) – for its willingness to engage with issues of political currency, doubts about its cinematic qualities were stoked by its speedy television premiere, a matter of months after its theatrical release.

It had also been some time since an independent film without US studio backing had performed as well as films of the last century like *The Full Monty*, and despite the eclecticism of the contemporary output, there was little that broke with established traditions of British filmmaking, and apparently 'no ground-breaking signature film such as *Performance* [1970] or *Trainspotting* about right now' (James 2007: 3).

Debates such as these have now become firmly embedded within commentary on contemporary British cinema in the UK. Industrial and creative developments have been closely monitored by the British print and broadcasting media, as well as by the academic community. In recent times, the conflicted nature of this commentary will have done much to disorientate the impartial observer. In July 2007 many newspapers reported the claims by John Woodward, the chief executive of the UK Film Council, that the 'British film industry seems to be firing on all cylinders' (Higgins 2007). Proof of an economic upturn was offered by the Council's statistical study of 2006, which trumpeted how the industry contributed over £4 billion to the economy (up 39 per cent on 2004) and noted the UK share of worldwide box-office takings was 8.5 per cent, 'equal to approximately five hundred million admissions'.[2]

But talk of revival was met with scepticism. Stephen Frears, director of *The Queen*, described the British film industry as 'leaderless' without the support of cultural impresarios to lobby on its behalf (see Brooks 2007), and Geoffrey Macnab used the absence of British films in competition at that year's Cannes Film Festival (the first time this had happened since 2001) to lament a cinema that was increasingly 'producer-led rather than director-led' (2007a) and unsupportive of bold, original voices working in the cultural sector. Like many commentators, Macnab took issue with both the 'selective use of statistics' and the perpetual grumblings of producers, coming to the conclusion that the picture remained more 'muddied' (see 2007b) than either would suggest.

Whilst the UK Film Council's published study indicated how nearly all UK studio films gained an international theatrical release in 2006, it also noted that this was only the case for 57 per cent of independent UK films. The revelation that the 'strongest UK film at the worldwide box office' that year was the Hollywood blockbuster *The Da Vinci Code* (2006) – only partly set in Britain – also seemed at odds with the praise elsewhere in the same document for films that projected 'strong images of cultural and national identity', with characters that 'help define Britishness for a wide audience'.

What is a British film?

The question of what exactly constitutes a British film continues to bother politicians, journalists and academics, but it has been a particularly pressing concern for filmmakers wishing to take advantage of UK funding schemes and tax relief strategies. According to the Films Act of 1985, which set out provisions to determine whether or not a film was 'British' enough to qualify for certain grants, 92.5 per cent of the running time had to be created in the UK, the production had to employ a labour force largely made up of UK citizens and the film had to be made by a company registered in the UK.

In 2007, this was superseded by the government's Cultural Test, which established more stringent criteria.[3] This set out a points system, divided into four sections – cultural content, cultural contribution, cultural hubs and cultural practitioners – across which a film had to score 16 out of a possible 31 available points. Almost half of the points were concentrated on the cultural 'content' section, with four points awarded each for a UK setting, British lead characters, British subject material and dialogue recorded mainly in English. The other sections rewarded the representation of 'diverse British culture, British heritage or British creativity', the filming or basing of the production in the UK and the involvement of British creative personnel (director, actors, key staff and so forth).

Writing in the *Telegraph* newspaper, then-MP Boris Johnson expressed the befuddlement of some politicians at this convoluted piece of legislation:

> You might have assumed that a 'British film' was a relatively straightforward concept. A British car is, broadly speaking, a car made in Britain. A British cheese is a cheese made in a British dairy. A British film is therefore a film made in the UK. (Johnson 2006)

Taken out of its immediate, industrial framework, the Department of Culture, Media and Sport's points system does indeed appear to be an absurd and unhelpful act of institutional over-complication, only confirming the point – taken for granted by most filmgoers and critics – that quantifying Britishness is a pointless endeavour. Nevertheless, it does draw attention to the problems of assessing cultural relevancy.

A case could be made for including Hollywood blockbusters such as *Charlie and the Chocolate Factory* (2005), *Nanny McPhee* (2005), *The Saint* (1997), *The Avengers* (1998), *King Arthur* (2004), *Beowulf* (2007) and the Harry Potter series (2001–) under a generous umbrella of British cinema. They are taken from British source material (history, novels and television shows), feature British performers and many were partly filmed in the UK. But whilst their claim to Britishness may have been integral to their promotion and appeal, it is a moot point whether any of these have any relevance to contemporary British society in the manner of, say, *This is England*, Shane Meadows' film about Midlands skinhead culture in the 1980s. It is perhaps fanciful, for example, to make a claim for the Harry Potter films as an exploration of the British class and school system, and far more useful to discuss them, along with other adaptations of British fantasy novels like the *Lord of the Rings* trilogy (2001–2003) and *The Golden Compass* (2007), as manifestations of global trends in the entertainment industry. The definition of a British film is further complicated by the proliferation of Hindi- and English-language Bollywood productions making use of British locations, and addressing both nationally specific and diasporic audiences (including some in the UK).

At the same time, there is a compelling argument for classifying the work of certain UK-based directors or screenwriters as British, even when connections to indigenous culture or geography are tenuous. Certainly within British film culture, and the commentary around it, there is a marked desire to bend the categorisation of British cinema so as to incorporate the likes of Paul Greengrass's *United 93*, Terence Davies's New York-set but Glasgow-filmed *The House of Mirth* (2000), Ken Loach's *Bread and Roses*

(2000), Michael Winterbottom's *In This World* (2002) and *Code 46* (2003), Kevin Macdonald's *The Last King of Scotland* and Danny Boyle's *Sunshine*.

In 2004, the British-born Asif Kapadia's feudal epic *The Warrior* (2001), set and filmed in Northern India, and with dialogue in Hindi, was named Best British Film at the British Academy of Film and Television Awards (BAFTA). However, in the previous year, when put forward by the Academy to represent the UK in the Best Foreign Language Film category at the Academy Awards, the film – a co-production between British, French, German and Indian companies, with funding from British Screen – was rejected for not being sufficiently 'British'.

Regardless of their funding, or the primary locations of filming, the inclusion of these films in an 'imagined community' (see Anderson 1991) of British cinema speaks of a desire to identify a cosmopolitan, auteur-led film culture, free from its former insularity of subject material and geographical focus, and a leader in formal and stylistic innovation.

Critical approaches

The upsurge of scholarly interest in contemporary UK filmmaking is in some respects illustrative of the robustness of British film studies as an academic field, as the plethora of journal articles, conferences, anthologies, monographs and PhD theses on the subject would attest. The journals *Screen*, *Cineaste* and the more recently established *Journal of British Film and Television* regularly carry articles responding to contemporary British film culture.

Furthermore, these responses have been more immediate than those to the filmmaking of previous eras. It was not until the early 1990s that rigorous evaluation of the output of the Thatcher period took place (see Friedman 1993), whereas monographs on the cinema of the Blair era by the likes of Paul Dave (2006) and Steve Blandford (2007) were published before the Prime Minister left office. Undoubtedly, British cinema's much-discussed renaissance of the late 1990s has been a generative factor. British film studies seems energised by the increasing number of texts with which to engage, and the intensification of the arguments around them.

Academic responses to contemporary British cinema have been broad-ranging and inter-disciplinary, underlining the diverse ways in which a national film culture might be understood and contextualised. At the moment, work being carried out within the bustling arena of British film studies relating to modern developments tends to fall into one of four broad (and admittedly overlapping) projects.

Firstly, there has been a critical tendency to situate recent films and trends within the broader history of British cinema, as exemplified by chronological and thematic surveys by Street (1997), Leach (2004) and Sargeant (2005). Also part of this trend are the many books and anthologies focusing on the evolution of particular genres, such as the horror film (Chibnall & Petley 2001), the 'heritage' film (Monk & Sargeant 2002; Higson 2003; Pidduck 2007), the historical film (Chapman 2005), the comedy-drama (Mather 2006), social realism (Lay 2002), the crime film (Chibnall & Murphy 1999) and the musical (Donnelly 2007; Mundy 2007).

A different pathway through British film history is offered by the strand of criticism which acknowledges the role of its key creative personnel, and its directors in particular. This not only encompasses studies of the work of notable auteurs such as Ken Loach (Leigh 2002), Mike Leigh (Watson 2004; Whitehead 2007) and Michael Winterbottom (Sinyard & Williams 2002) but reference guides to British directors (Allon *et al.* (eds) 2001; Murphy 2006; Shail 2007).

An emphasis on the political, cultural and geographical applications of the national cinema defines a third critical approach. This area of study is particularly lively, and it dovetails with the recent interrogation of the 'national' in film and cultural studies more generally. As shall be discussed in the following chapter, the very notion of a coherent indigenous cinema has been thoroughly problematised within film studies, and the conversation about the validity of the national as a critical tool has been continued, rather than ignored, by studies of the cinematic output of the countries that make up the United Kingdom. This includes work by Dave (2006) on English cinema, McLoone (2000), Barton (2004) and Hill (2006) on Irish cinema, Petrie (2000) on Scottish cinema and Blandford (2007) on the significance of the regional 'break-up' of Britain on its contemporary film culture.

This scrutiny of regionalism and its political and industrial implications has often taken place within a broader European or international context. Case studies of British films and cities have been included in surveys of the continental cinema (see, for example, Mazierska & Rascaroli 2002), and the affiliation and exchanges between British and European film cultures have been the subject of a number of academic conferences that have taken place in the UK and beyond in recent years. Scholars of the 'smaller' cinemas of the British Isles – in other words, Welsh and Scottish filmmaking – have compared these with equivalent 'peripheral' cinemas worldwide (see Hjort & Petrie 2007), and there has also been an interest in the specificities of 'space and place' within British film, such as Charlotte Brunsdon's study of cinematic London (2007).

A fourth area of academic attention is the workings of the British film industry itself (see chapter 2). Driven by a pressing need to historicise and contest the role of government-backed organisations like the UK Film Council, the analysis can sometimes be arid and speculative. But it also has a polemical quality often lacking in accounts of British cinema, and ranges from despair over the sorry state of British filmmaking to more practical suggestions about the future of the industry.

Although this amounts to a comprehensive resource for the study of contemporary British cinema, there are still areas where the film scholar seems reluctant to venture. Some critical gaps have been plugged, however, through research undertaken beyond the immediate terrain of British film studies. Literary and historical scholars have considered the implications of adaptation and historical recreation, particularly with regard to period or 'heritage' films. Insights have also come by way of those working primarily in the fields of sociology, geography and media theory who have used filmic examples of representation (for example, of sexuality, gender, ethnicity, class and of particular regions and cities) to illustrate their analyses of cultural identity or to consider the interrelationship between the film and tourist industries.

However, substantial work remains to be done on the symbioses between British cinema and other forms of media, most notably television and the Internet, as well as its relationship to (sub)cultural phenomena such as music, sport, fashion and videogaming. The convergence of media in the twenty-first century is producing new models of production and reception that have implications for the way that audiences engage with British cinema. Increasingly, web resources such as search engines, blogs, message boards, fan-sites, video-sharing sites, social networking sites and the Internet Movie Database (IMDb) provide an alternate means of gauging the impact of British films and filmmakers, as well as promoting them.

In an important article written in 1986, Julian Petley suggested that studies of British cinema thus far had valorised filmmaking in the documentary realist mode, and that films of a non-realist vein constituted a 'lost continent'. There has undoubtedly been progress since then, but the inclination to prioritise 'respectable' films over popular genre cinema may explain the relative lack of attention given, for instance, to the rebirth of the British horror cinema in the 2000s.

The quantity of films now being produced gives ample scope for the identification of representational trends, generic similarities and auteurist strategies. But the sheer volume of texts to consider only complicates the task of deciding what is significant and worthy of scrutiny. Responses to contemporary cultural phenomena inevitably lack the benefit of hindsight, and future considerations of the cinematic output of the Blair years may call attention to aspects not yet fully noted or processed by contemporaneous scholars (or audiences). It will also be easier, in due course, to position films of the era within the various oeuvres of their creative personnel. Furthermore, the canon of 'significant' texts that emerges from recent scholarship may also undergo adjustment with critical distance.

Whilst the current work on British film culture is undeniably wide-ranging, given the hazards of reacting to current developments, analyses so far of British cinema in the period between 1997 and 2008 have quickly established a consensus of opinion on what should constitute the corpus of study. Popular films like *The Full Monty* and *East is East* (1999), which happened to chime with the preoccupations of cultural critics and commentators, are rightly given due attention, but there are many intriguing examples of filmmaking, such as the rural-set *The Darkest Light* (1999) and the English road movie *Heartlands* (2002), that have mostly gone beneath the critical radar, presumably because they do not make a neat fit with established academic paradigms.

If critical work on British film history has often been reluctant to make explicit value judgements, the analysis of contemporary cinema has generally been more opinionated. Neutrality is less easy to observe when the film culture is in development, and the debates around it are still topical and divisive. However, there is still a tendency to contextualise and explain rather than to evaluate *cinematic* worth. Pertinent aspects that are all too often overlooked in studies of the national cinema include the creative deployment of genre, the level of artistic ambition, the ways in which the British landscape is rendered familiar or unfamiliar, and the distinctive qualities of performance, *mise-en-scène*, cinematography and sound.

Other than in the form of longer review essays, close textual responses to contemporary cinema are still frustratingly rare, no doubt because this approach is often deemed (wrongly) to be a denial of the multiple influences on modern film culture.

The academic significance now awarded to the study of contemporary British film culture is underlined by its permeation through all sectors of post-16 education in the UK, a situation unthinkable twenty years ago, and a testimony to the vibrancy and breadth of scholarly activity in the field. There are dozens of courses pertaining to current British cinema in colleges and universities in Britain and beyond, and a small industry of publications and online resources geared towards guiding teachers and lecturers through the terrain. Again, there is a danger that the immediate enshrinement of particular films as 'set texts', simply because they coincide with contemporary issues of cultural concern, may work to close off other avenues of critical engagement.

2   INDUSTRY AND CULTURE

The British film industry

The cocktail of bombast and critique that has served as coverage of the British film industry will be wearyingly familiar even to those with only a passing knowledge of its perpetual cycles of boom and bust or its history of muddled government intervention. The British film business tends to be characterised as a fragmentary cottage industry of small, undercapitalised independent companies, which now and again enjoy a one-off commercial breakthrough. Unable to match Hollywood's systems of vertical integration, the British film business has historically struggled to distribute and market its films.

However, in the mid-1990s hopes for a renaissance were prompted by a clutch of home-grown hits and anticipation of a supportive Labour government. There had been similar optimism in the 1980s, when a series of critical and commercial successes, and the arrival of Channel Four as a key source of funding, seemed destined to revitalise British cinema after a decade of near-disastrous inertia. However, the calamitous collapse of Goldcrest Films – responsible for works such as *Local Hero* (1983) and *Hope and Glory* (1987) – would subsequently make investors wary.

Cinema and the state

Today, funding for British filmmaking emanates from a variety of sources: UK television companies, European and international companies operating in the UK, Hollywood film companies, European initiatives such as the European Union's MEDIA programme, as well as private investment. However, public subsidies also play a significant role, and indeed no history of British cinema would be complete without a consideration of the government's track record of intervention and protectionism.

At the heart of the debates around the British film industry lies a philosophical dilemma about state funding. Opinion differs as to whether direct grants to particular films, or 'slates' of productions, are more effective in bringing about prosperity than the provision of tax breaks, or indeed whether public money should even be spent on film at all. There is also the question of what kind of films to fund: commercial ventures or those that are otherwise unlikely to be made in a market-driven industry. Phil Wickham summarises the situation thus:

> If you fund films that large numbers of people wish to see and that will do well at the box office there may be some return to the exchequer (and ultimately the taxpayer) but if they are going to make money wouldn't the industry make them anyway? As [Alexander] Walker points out this could lead to citizens funding already profitable businesses. (2003: 15)

However, should the state support non-commercial ventures, the majority will then be contributing to work that only a minority may find to their liking.

In the mid-1990s, radical changes to systems of public funding were afoot. Proposals for the investment of money from the National Lottery were made by John Major's Conservative government in 1996, and carried through the following year by the Labour Culture Secretary, Chris Smith. Three franchises (DNA Film Ltd, The Film Consortium and Pathé Productions), each comprising film production, distribution and sales companies, were awarded six-year contracts and a share of £90 million of Lottery money. The purpose behind offering substantial grants to these 'mini-studios' was to encourage investment and profitability in the long term.

The immediate result was to increase the production of mid-budget, commercially-minded films, but early signs were not promising, and press scrutiny unsparing (Alexander Walker, of the *Evening Standard*, was particularly dogged in his criticism of public money squandered on poorly performing films). By 2003, the companies had produced 44 films, far less than anticipated, including box-office flops such as *Janice Beard 45 WPM* (1999) and *Strictly Sinatra* (2001) and some critical and commercial successes like *Ratcatcher* (1999) and *28 Days Later* (2002).

In April 2000, amidst much fanfare, the UK Film Council was set up by the Department of Culture, Media and Sport as an umbrella organisation for all of the main public funding institutions, with a rationale to oversee all facets of the UK industry and to develop and endorse British film culture; it also took over responsibility for the dispersal of Lottery funding. The Film Council's first public statement of aims and objectives clarified that part of their remit was to 'facilitate the production of popular British theatrical films which are profitable and attract significant audiences at home and abroad' (UK Film Council 2000: 14). The emphasis was on the promotion of a range of filmmaking, but for many the rhetoric was dismayingly commercial and script-centred. Concerns were also raised about the investment of National Lottery funds in commercial filmmaking, the partnership of public body and private funding being a typically Blairite arrangement.

The second aspect of government intervention to impact upon British filmmaking was the provision of generous tax incentives. In his inaugural budget of 1997, Chancellor Gordon Brown approved a hundred per cent tax write-off on production and acquisition costs for British films with budgets of up to £15 million. By permitting filmmakers to recoup their investment earlier, this measure had the result of reducing budgets, but the loopholes provided by complex sale-and-leaseback schemes also gave wealthy investors a means of tax avoidance. Undoubtedly, tax incentives contributed to the late-1990s production boom, as well as the attractiveness of the UK as a filming location for Hollywood productions, leading to doubts about whether this was quite the same thing as a renaissance in the cultural sense.

In 2004, word of imminent changes to the tax rules gave a jolt to the industry. There followed a period of confusion and transition in which anxieties were aired, on the one hand, about wealthy investors benefiting from the British taxpayer, and, on the other hand, the removal of any incentive for Hollywood blockbusters to film in the UK should the system be tightened. The old system was ended as of April 2006, and a new tax credit scheme introduced allowing films that passed the British 'cultural test' (see chapter 1) and cost under £20 million to claim back a quarter of their costs (up to a maximum of twenty per cent of their total budget). However, unlike the previous tax breaks which applied to productions made anywhere in the world, the new system stipulated that these only applied to UK expenditure. An announcement in summer 2007 that the 22nd film in the James Bond franchise would be made at Pinewood Studios was received as a sign that these developments had not driven Hollywood away from the UK.

The industry and television

The British film industry also continues to be propped up by the filmmaking activities of UK television channels, for the most part acting as mini-studios supervising the journey from script development to international theatrical distribution (and eventual television broadcast). BSkyB and ITV have had modest involvement, but Film Four (the filmmaking wing of Channel Four) and BBC Films, despite undergoing restructuring in recent years, remain key players through their patronage of titles such as the BBC's *A Way of Life* (2004) and Film Four's *The Last King of Scotland*.

Having established a reputation for politically committed and creatively challenging work in the 1980s, Film Four would pursue a more commercial path in the subsequent decade, in keeping with the parent channel's gradual shift away from its original remit for minority-orientated or alternative material. No longer merely the production and development arm of Channel Four, with a commitment only to supporting talent and producing films for television, Film Four was expanded into a fully integrated company with an eye on the international market.

Although some of Film Four's earlier films – like *Trainspotting* and *East is East* – had quickly became canonical, a string of mid-budget failures around the turn of the decade, such as *Charlotte Gray* (2001) and *Lucky Break* (2001), would lead to a scaling down of operations. The incorporation of Film Four back within the parent channel in 2002, together with its refocus on lower budget, in-house movies, 'marked a symbolic moment: the end of the mini-boom and perhaps of the mini-studio concept' (Macnab 2002: 18). Within a few years, Film Four had returned, with some success, to its original policy of supporting indigenously relevant or politically provocative material such as *This is England* and *The Road to Guantánamo* (2006).

The industry in the twenty-first century

Economic and technological developments, such as the rise of digital formats and online distribution, may pose a challenge to the global film industry in the new millennium, but they also offer new opportunities. Neil Watson argues that a flourishing British film industry can only take shape through the 'creation of fully integrated companies, capable of producing both films and television programmes on a consistent basis, and able to exploit aggressively the markets opened by the increasing convergence between the television, computer and telecommunications industries' (2000: 86). A similar conclusion is reached by Bill Baillieu and John Goodchild, who suggest that too much attention has been paid to the 'cultural and creative aspects of filmmaking, rather than the business of selling films to audiences' (2002: 151). These sentiments encapsulate the differing prioritisations given to economic and artistic imperatives in debates about British cinema, as well as the desire for convergence between business and creativity.

Lessons have been learned from the fate of both Film Four and PolyGram Filmed Entertainment (PFE). In the 1990s, PFE became the UK's most successful production company, backing a string of profitable films, including (through its subsidiary Working Title) *Four Weddings and a Funeral*, *Fargo* (1996) and *Bean* (1997) (see Kuhn 2002). When PFE was sold by its parent company and merged with Universal Pictures at the turn of the century, its passing was regarded by some as self-inflicted, having 'expanded too quickly, opening costly distribution arms in a dozen countries' (Macnab 2002: 20).

The dilemma faced by PFE and Film Four, and indeed the industry as a whole, was similar: 'do you make big-budget international films with the studios and risk falling on your face or do you make smaller films basically for domestic consumption?' (ibid.). The former strategy had been promoted in a provocative speech delivered in 2002 by the filmmaker Alan Parker, then Chairman of the UK Film Council. Parker urged the abandonment of 'the "Little England" vision of a UK industry comprised of small British film companies delivering parochial British films' (quoted in Chanan 2004: 109). According to Parker, this 'British' industry had never really existed, and 'in the brutal age of global capitalism, it never will' (ibid.).

Parker's selective vision was vociferously challenged by critics and filmmakers. For Alex Cox, this was an 'outrageous proposal based on imaginary premises' (2004: 113), seemingly oblivious to the major contributions to British film culture made by small independent companies (such as Bryanston Films in the early 1960s). Cox was not alone in arguing that the health of the British film industry could be determined as much by its breadth of aspiration as by its reach, its success locatable in its relevance to native audiences as much as through its global attractiveness. Still, Parker's claims were not utterly dismissed. Although in disagreement with Parker's dismissal of the 'parochial' as a potential source of great art, Phil Wickham agreed that there had never been a 'real film industry in the UK of any influence – rather that great talent and great films have occasionally emerged in spite, rather than because of the structures around them' (2003: 17).

The emergence of structures like the UK Film Council brought academics as well as industry professionals into a conversation about British cinema's relation to 'broader, European and global economic, political and aesthetic structures' (Street 2005: 86). Issues of policy and its impact upon the cultural sector formed part of the debate generated by the Independent Film Parliament, a 'consultative forum for pluralism and diversity' that first met in July 2003 and subsequently had its proceedings reported in *Vertigo* magazine and the inaugural issue of the *Journal of British Film and Television*.[1] Sarah Street's coverage of a *Screen*-sponsored symposium on British film policy in February 2004 noted how recent developments in government policy had engendered a 'culture of interrogation that we might learn from past mistakes and try to overcome some of the industry's historical and more recent problems' (ibid.).

British film culture: towards the mainstream?

One of the most remarkable features of British film culture of the 1990s was its sheer plenitude:

> … more British films (over a hundred per year from 1996), more money to make them, more screens (1,685 in 1990, 2,383 in 1997), more cinemagoers (97.37 million in 1990, 139.3 million in 1997), more educational courses, more media outlets for film promotion and reviewing. (Brown 2000: 28)

Yet quantity alone could not provide an automatically supportive climate for a perpetually fragile, haphazard industry to prosper, not least because far more films were now being made than being seen. Indeed, in the early years of the new millennium, it was 'still possible to make some of the same sweeping generalisations about British cinema one could have made fifty years ago' (McFarlane 2001: 273). Commercial breakthroughs were still rare, and many of the movies being made conformed to stereotypical expectations of a talky, male-centred, class-bound cinema. Its reliance upon other indigenous cultural forms such as literature, theatre and television for stories and talent was nothing new, and the relationship with European and Hollywood film cultures remained as complex as ever.

Although the parameters and aspirations of British film culture are largely unchanged, it is nevertheless possible to discern a gradual shift to the middle ground in recent British filmmaking, a development broadly in line with a New Labour ideology that prioritises target attainment over creativity. In practical terms alone, the market-orientated funding policies of the Blair years have done much to foster the populist aims of film production.

This 'mainstreaming' of the film culture is discernible in various ways. It can be witnessed in the de-politicisation of attitude by filmmakers who may once have used the medium to explore aspects of identity politics in a more formally complex manner. Stories concerning the experiences of non-mainstream groups, such as British Asians, tend now to be addressed to a broad audience, thus diluting – some would say – their purpose of speaking to and for a particular societal group (see chapter 4). It can also be seen in the revival of certain popular genres, such as the horror and gangster film, and in the greater professionalism shown by filmmakers in their appreciation of how to target and market their work (see chapter 3). This mainstreaming of attitude is also apparent from the imposition of unexpectedly upbeat endings onto material associated with a social realist tradition more accustomed to tragic conclusions. *Billy Elliot* may pay direct homage to Ken Loach's *Kes* (1969), another tale of a talented boy doomed to a life of manual toil in a northern town, but the difference between the crowd-pleasing ending of the former, and the bleak, matter-of-fact conclusion of the latter, could not be greater. *Billy Elliot* is thus emblematic of the realist-flavoured film's newfound propensity for efficient denouements that obey the standard requirements of classical Hollywood narrative.

This mainstreaming trend poses a critical challenge to the traditional definitions of British cinema in terms of polarising tendencies. A distinction between 'realism and tinsel' – a phrase originating with producer Michael

Balcon, and utilised by Robert Murphy (1992) in relation to British cinema of the 1940s – has been used to convey, firstly, Britain's relationship to US film culture, and, secondly, the divergent currents of socially-responsive filmmaking and more fanciful types of storytelling in British cinema. However, as exemplified by hybrid films such as the underclass thriller *Dirty Pretty Things* (2002), these binaries are losing their usefulness. Likewise, a supposed schism between traditions of respectable and unrespectable filmmaking – with literary adaptations and social realist films exemplifying the former, and popular genre films the latter – is problematised by the contemporary impulse towards convergence. Of course, far from being an exclusively British trait, the blurring of high and low culture is symptomatic of postmodern culture more generally.

Whilst the so-called respectable forms of filmmaking have been given a more populist makeover, a tradition of 'distasteful' cinema – whether of visual flamboyance, provocation or basic cheapness, as exemplified by the Hammer horror films or the iconoclastic work of Ken Russell – has largely been suppressed, emerging only occasionally through low-budget horror/exploitation films like *Sacred Flesh* (2000) and *Cradle of Fear* (2001) or vigilante films such as *Outlaw* (2007). In their analysis of the career of the prolific but commercially unpopular director Michael Winterbottom, Neil Sinyard and Melanie Williams (2002) draw attention to the various qualities of his work that place him beyond the mainstream of British film culture. These include the 'un-English look' of the films and their engagement with areas of contemporary society ignored elsewhere, but also the uniqueness of their 'emotional bravura' in an otherwise weak-blooded cinema most associated with irony and 'sardonic cynicism' (2002: 114).

The decline of the cultural film?

Within contemporary British cinema there is a healthy roll-call of idiosyncratic filmmakers pursuing adventurous styles and subject matter rather than purely commercial goals. Directors (and in some cases writer/directors) such as Michael Winterbottom, Danny Boyle, Mike Figgis, Sara Sugarman, Penny Woolcock, Mark Herman, David Kane, Alex Cox, Christine Edzard, Julien Temple and Gilles MacKinnon have all produced distinctive work, despite having to work within, around or even beyond an unsupportive industry. However, some observers of British film culture have expressed concern about the lack of new, innovative filmmakers to keep alive the flame of cultural or experimental cinema in the twenty-first century, whilst also lamenting a hostile funding climate that has slowed down the work rate of respected auteurs such as Terence Davies and Lynne Ramsay.

Within film scholarship, a distinction is sometimes drawn between avant-garde practices – usually occurring beyond the mainstream structures of funding, production and exhibition, and typically involving a questioning of the medium itself – and a tradition of (European) art cinema that challenges narrative and stylistic convention but is distributed via traditional outlets. The British filmmakers normally cited as evidence of a hybridising phenomenon, in that their films incorporate experimental impulses within the more 'mainstream' parameters of the art film, are Peter Greenaway, Derek Jarman, Sally Potter and Terence Davies (see O'Pray 1996). All came to prominence as feature filmmakers in the 1980s, and were in the main sustained throughout the decade by the patronage of Channel Four television, with its commitment to oppositional voices and stories.

The perceived marginalisation of these particular talents – whose highly personal work had been recognised by international art-house audiences – was deemed in some quarters to be a threat to the cultural prestige of the national cinema. Sally Potter's cross-cultural love story *Yes* (2004), spoken entirely in iambic pentameter, has a formal rigour and earnestness – some might say humourlessness – rare in contemporary British cinema. However, the inability of Terence Davies, one of the UK's most distinguished directors, to secure finance for his next project after *The House of Mirth* (2000), the poetic documentary *Of Time and the City* (2008), offers an indication of how the independent sector would be ill-served by the populist agenda of the funding bodies in the 2000s.

Peter Greenaway's reputation as a maverick railing against the limitations of mainstream filmmaking was established in the 1970s and 1980s through a stylised and painterly series of experimental shorts and feature films. Seemingly frustrated with traditional film formats, and indeed the state of cinema *per se*, Greenaway's work since the 1990s has been dominated by international multi-media projects, such as the ambitious *Tulse Luper Suitcases* project (2003–) – described as a personal history of Uranium – and encompassing films, theatrical events, installations and online activities. As a 'database filmmaker' (Manovich 2001: xxiv), less interested in narrative than in processes of collection and categorisation, Greenaway's strategies happen to bear relation to the preoccupations of recent media theorists. To some a visionary, to others a pompous obscurist using the latest technologies to feed his encyclopaedic obsessions, Greenaway's recent output – awkward to distribute and consume, let alone critically engage with – has generally passed beneath the critical and industrial radar.

In an article written in 2006, Ryan Gilbey claimed that a 'coherent British art-house scene' (2006: 41) – as epitomised by Jarman, Greenway and Davies – had petered out by the turn of the century. For Gilbey, the decline of this tradition can be traced back to the commercial success of films such as *The Full Monty* that persuaded the industry to focus its energies on perfecting formulas for box-office achievement. Whilst the 'coherence' of the 1980s films is open to question – they shared a broadly similar political impulse but little else – Gilbey is right to draw attention to the cumulative impact that they had upon critics and audiences. In successive decades there have been equivalent pockets of experimental activity, but the number of active practitioners has gradually dwindled, and the films themselves have become steadily harder to fund, categorise and access.

However, a cluster of mid-1990s work by directors sharing an experimental background and certain conceptual preoccupations gave hope for the arrival of a new wave of British art cinema. Patrick Keiller's *London* (1994) and *Robinson in Space* (1997), Andrew Kötting's *Gallivant* (1997) and *This Filthy Earth* (2001) and John Maybury's *Love is the Devil* (1998) are arresting films that blur the boundaries between fiction and documentary, experimental and art cinema.

Patrick Keiller's films of the 1990s have been explained as 'fictionalised documentaries, blending the picaresque narrative, the documentary portrait and the filmed essay' (Dave 2000: 339). Consisting entirely of static images of decaying urban spaces and manufacturing industries, *London* and *Robinson in Space* form a polemical two-part project in which the capital, and then the whole of Britain, is re-imagined from the perspective of the fictional *flâneur* Robinson, and his travelling companion, an unseen narrator (voiced by Paul Schofield). Kötting's *Gallivant* describes a more personal quest, the filmmaker's clockwise jaunt around the coastline of Britain with his grandmother and daughter. Like Keiller's films, it is infused with imagery of decay and erosion, but in contrast to their somnolent pacing and metronomic rhythms, Kötting's journey round the island's liminal spaces is told through a dense, haphazard collage of inserts, tangents, time-lapses and interviews. However, as Claire Smith suggests, Kötting and Keiller's work share a 'primacy of landscape over script, the possibility of fortuitous connections between the act of filming and the subject, a sense of getting one over on the institutions, and a DIY approach' (2000: 154).

In the 2000s, this tradition of nonconformist feature films has been sustained through the quirky, loosely-plotted work of Ben Hopkins and John Hardwick. The appearance of Andrew Kötting in small acting roles in films by both directors gives a pleasing linearity to the evolution of cultural filmmaking, but also an indication of its insularity and narrowness of company in the new millennium.

Having made clear his frustration with an unsupportive industry, Hopkins would follow his films *Simon Magus* (1999) and *The Nine Lives of Tomas Katz* (2000) with documentaries made outside of the UK. *The Nine Lives of Tomas Katz* is an absurdist apocalyptic fantasy suffused with parochial references to British culture, with a deadpan humour reminiscent of the televisual comedy of Monty Python and Chris Morris. But it also seems at times like a parody of the defamiliarising tactics and improvisatory methods found in the films of Kötting and Keiller, and the collaborative work of Christopher Petit and Ian Sinclair. Featuring a protean character (played by Tom Fisher) that constantly changes identity throughout the narrative, the film mischievously represents the capital as a 'city built on a mystic network', where 'even the bollards can have powers' and the underground system is used to 'ferry the dead to the valley of the last judgement'.

An unsettling underworld is also evoked in John Hardwick's circular, dream-like *33x Around the Sun* (2005). An amnesiac wakes up in a deserted hospital and roams the nocturnal streets of an eerily deserted city in search of clarity, meeting a series of oddball characters along the way, before his journey returns him to his place of origin. The casting of the German-born Lars Rudolph as the disorientated wanderer provides a connecting thread with the British experimental film's fascination with exilic characters adrift in an unfamiliar landscape; a theme that has spilled over into popular genre filmmaking such as *28 Days Later* and *Creep* (2004). Psychological dislocation and transformed landscapes are also defining

Psychological dislocation and transformed landscapes: Lars Rudolph as the nocturnal wanderer of *33x Around the Sun*

features of character-driven films such as *Morvern Callar* (2002) and *Young Adam* (2003) that fall more readily within the category of art-house cinema rather than avant-garde practice, despite being for the most part visually-orientated instead of narrative driven.

Conceptual and community films

If some have proposed a decline in British cultural cinema, recent years have also witnessed the rise to prominence of a group of young British artists – such as Gillian Wearing, Sam Taylor-Wood and Steve McQueen – who have used film and video in their installation pieces, sometimes drawing upon popular genres and modes of storytelling, but usually for abstract or ambient purpose.

Occasional convergences between the mainstream film industry and the conceptual modes of contemporary art have borne strange fruit. Tracey Emin's *Top Spot* (2004), a semi-autobiographical account of her wayward adolescence in Margate, has the loose, artisinal quality of her gallery work, and aspires no further than to be a continuation of it. British filmmakers have also exploited the possibilities of utilising multiple screens as a method of storytelling. The division of the screen into a triptych of different perspectives in Duncan Roy's *AKA* (2002) adds little to the experience other than a vague sense of the central protagonist's unstable identity, whilst Mike Figgis's eccentric *Hotel* (2001) incorporates and augments the split-screen experimentation of his 'real-time' *Timecode* (2000). Simon Pummell's *Bodysong* (2003) uses archive footage to plot the human life cycle, from conception and childhood, through the rituals of adulthood to death; suggestions of man's predetermination for violence and chaos are effectively counterposed with images of creativity and rebirth.

Then again, these images of regeneration may be wishful thinking for those hopeful of a young generation of filmmakers on the horizon with the mixture of entrepreneurial ambition and individualistic vision necessary to revitalise the British cultural film in the digital age. Technological advances have in theory opened up new possibilities of production and distribution for oppositional voices, but their alienation from the mainstream has never been so keenly felt.

The problems of marginality are exemplified by the fate of recent films made by the Amber Collective, an independent group of filmmakers based in the North East of England. One of the last remaining members of the workshop movement that flourished in the 1980s under the patronage of Channel Four television, Amber have increasingly struggled to promote their formally experimental films about the plight of working-class communities. Described in one review as a 'genuine treasure, worth ten of *Billy Elliot*' (Kelly 2001: 44), their film *Like Father* (2001) was given a UK television broadcast, as much of their previous work had been. But their digitally-filmed *Shooting Magpies* (2005) has bypassed traditional channels of exhibition entirely, and at the time of writing is only available directly from the website of the filmmakers. A couple of years after its release, the film had generated little in the way of Internet 'noise' (critical and fan reviews and so forth) but, like many independent filmmakers, Amber seem resigned to the haphazard afterlife of their work.

British cinema and Hollywood

US investment has undoubtedly kept the British film industry afloat over the years, just as British creative and technical talent have contributed greatly to Hollywood film culture. But the lopsided nature of Anglo-American relations has been playfully acknowledged across numerous comedies and capers, be it through the very title of Ronny Yu's *The 51st State* (2001) or the storylines of *The Big Tease* (1999), *Wimbledon* (2004) and *The Calcium Kid* (2004) about competition entrants or sporting underdogs triumphing against powerful American opponents. In British cinema, cultural and economic deference to Hollywood is so ingrained that it is often felt to pose a threat to the individuality of British film culture and its capacity to reflect national concerns. For example, Nick James (2001) explains how the funding bodies' disinclination for risk results in formulaic screenplays, reliance upon star casting and compromised material. This sentiment is echoed by Mike Wayne, who uses a case study of the 'mid-Altantic' tactics of Working Title and its production of *Billy Elliot* to illustrate how 'the integration and subordination of British cinema into Hollywood and the American market provides massively diminished conditions within which British filmmakes could explore the diversity and complexity of life within the United Kingdom, whilst also functioning to magnify internal relations of domination' (2006a: 63).

The migration of British creative talent across the Atlantic, whether literally or figuratively, is hardly a new development, but it became apparent in the mid-1990s that many young British filmmakers were looking towards Hollywood for inspiration and, in some cases, a sustainable career along the lines of other successful émigrés such as Alfred Hitchcock and Ridley Scott. The mixed creative and commercial fortunes of Paul W. S. Anderson, Danny Cannon, Christopher Nolan, Danny Boyle and Jonathan Glazer demonstrate the hazards of taking on Hollywood at its own game with high-concept formulas, genre filmmaking or films designed as cult artefacts.

As well as a generator of directorial talent, British cinema of the 1990s and 2000s also launched the careers of a number of young actors and actresses, many of whom seem equally comfortable working on UK and US projects, and across a variety of genres. In this respect, they differ greatly from previous British performers who have tended to be defined principally by way of their nationality. For example, Hugh Grant, one of the most significant British stars to reach prominence in the early 1990s, has experienced difficulty operating outside of the romantic comedy genre and seems doomed to play variants on the bumbling English underachiever (see Spicer 2004). Likewise, Helena Bonham Carter, pushed into the spotlight through her work in the 1980s on Merchant-Ivory films, took some time to expand her career away from period dramas. In contrast, emerging talents such as Ewan McGregor, Samantha Morton, Daniel Craig, Jude Law, Andy Serkis, Christian Bale, Clive Owen, Orlando Bloom, Rhys Ifans, Kate Winslet – and, more recently, Keira Knightley, Jamie Bell and James McAvoy – have sustained careers that happily span Hollywood blockbusters, independent US cinema, relatively modest British films (and sometimes television) and auteur work by the likes of Peter Greenaway (McGregor), Lynne Ramsay (Morton), John Maybury (Craig) and Jane Campion (Winslet).

Transnational careers like these are now the norm, a testimony in some respects to the breadth of British cinema, and its attractiveness to those who might easily be absorbed within other film industries, but a reminder too of how a distinctly British star system has never really been tenable. Today there are few British stars with an easily definable and marketable persona. The most successful performers are those who have chameleon ruthlessness rather than the traditional star qualities of glamour or recurrent traits. Within British cinema, character actors abound (for example, Shirley Henderson, Bill Nighy and Sean Harris), but with the possible exception of 'laddish' presences like Nick Moran or Danny Dyer, few performers have come to prominence through an association with particular kinds of roles or subject matter.

Whilst some British actors have garnered success beyond the UK, the appearance of Hollywood stars in British productions has become familiar as a funding and promotional strategy. Notable examples of non-British actors with a proclivity for playing well-known historical and literary characters (and stirring up patriotic browbeating as a consequence) include Cate Blanchett (as Elizabeth I), Renée Zellweger (as Bridget Jones and Beatrix Potter), Gwyneth Paltrow (as Jane Austen's Emma), Anne Hathaway (playing Jane Austen herself) and Johnny Depp (as both J. M. Barrie and Sweeney Todd), whilst Samuel L. Jackson, Scarlett Johannson, Christina Ricci, Josh Hartnett and others have brought Hollywood slickness to British thrillers and comedies. In particular, Working Title has taken up the casting of American actresses in its romantic comedies as a kind of authorial signature. The strategy of casting international actors to perk up narratives of otherwise parochial interest is both demonstrated and satirised by the comedies *Churchill: The Hollywood Years* (2004) and *I Want Candy* (2007). The former parodies revisionist Hollywood versions of British history; in the latter, two penniless filmmakers hire a glamorous actress (played by Carmen Electra) to spice up their embarrassingly threadbare porn film.

When the Bristol-based Aardman Animation, famous for their painstaking 'stop-frame' work, struck a five-picture deal with DreamWorks Animation, the casting of Mel Gibson in *Chicken Run* (2000) as the voice of the American male hero amidst an otherwise British-centred story smacked of compromise. The unapologetically parochial accent of their subsequent film, *Wallace and Gromit: The Curse of the Were-Rabbit* (2005), may well have been a contributing factor in DreamWorks' subsequent termination of their contract.

The casting of American actors in British films has occasionally coincided with a diegetic interest in the interrelationship between US and UK film culture. In *Notting Hill* (1999), a mainstream American movie star, Anna Scott (played by Julia Roberts, one of the biggest box-office draws of the time), falls in love with a bookseller played by Hugh Grant, and thus with a culture – and a cinema – that is less demonstrative but posited as more authentic. Furthermore, the character swaps big-budget action movies for a 'heritage' film produced in the UK (a Henry James adaptation).

Interestingly, in *Love Actually* (2003), the film that completed a trilogy of comedies written by Richard Curtis, the Anglo-American romances of *Four Weddings and a Funeral* and *Notting Hill* were replaced by a broad range of courtships, and a few involved characters played by European actresses (Heike Makatsch, Lúcia Moniz) who were used prominently in the film's marketing campaigns across European territories. Furthermore, the depiction of the US president (played by Billy Bob Thornton) as a sleazy philanderer making assumptions about the willingness of the Prime Minister (played by Hugh Grant) to capitulate to his wishes struck a bullish political note at a moment when the Bush-Blair alignment on foreign policy was coming under considerable domestic scrutiny. A comic storyline concerning a British traveller, Colin (Kris Marshall), who is unfathomably attractive to sexy American girls seemed an acknowledgement that the narrative of Anglo-American romance was becoming exhausted. Placed alongside other Working Title productions of the late 2000s with European affiliations such as *Mr Bean's Holiday* and *Elizabeth: The Golden Age*, Curtis's film comes across as a belated recognition of the relevance of Britain's ties to Europe and its diverse film cultures.

British cinema and Europe

British film culture may have a 'semi-detached' relationship to European filmmaking (Nowell-Smith 2004: 53) but it is wrong to overlook the deep-rooted artistic, political and economic connections between British and continental cinema. The complexity of international production poses a challenge to the familiar paradigm that pits Hollywood cinema (whether US productions or films influenced by classical Hollywood models of film-making) against an auteur-led tradition of European art cinema. However, it is still possible to isolate British films which bear traces of a debt to this latter tradition through their formal and stylistic choices. For example, Emily Young's *Kiss of Life* (2003), an atmospheric exploration of family trauma, evokes memories of Krzysztof Kieślowski's later films, not entirely unexpectedly, since Young trained at the Polish National Film School. Within a national cinematic tradition that is, for the most part, stolidly dialogue-driven and literal-minded, filmmakers like Young, Lynne Ramsay, Pawel Pawlikowski and the Quay Brothers stand apart through their rare devotion to the primacy of the image. The languorous, ambivalent quality of their work renders it quite distinct – and not a little exotic – within the British context.

Although it is still feasible to describe a European sensibility in relation to auteurist traditions, the contours of contemporary European cinema are as resistant to mapping as the continent's own political and geographical boundaries. But even if European film culture, like that of the UK, has been utterly colonised by Hollywood – in that filmgoers have little to choose from other than US films – and in spite of the fact that European films rarely reach audiences beyond their place of origin, it is important to acknowledge the continental connections.

According to Wendy Everett, it is the very fragmentation of Europe and its cinema that is the root of its fascination. 'Movement across borders' (2005: 104) is not only a characteristic concern of European film, but the reason for its necessity: 'European films are open to a plurality of read-ings, are perpetually transformative in the open-ended personal journeys they offer, and thus capable of accelerating change, variety and difference' (ibid.).

Britain's bond with Europe is at its most visible in films that explore issues of relevance across the European political spectrum. Recurrent themes include asylum and economic migration, dealt with in *Dirty Pretty Things*, *In This World*, *Beautiful People* (1999), *Wondrous Oblivion* (2003) and *Gypo* (2005), and clashes between Western and Islamic cultures, examined by *My Son the Fanatic* (1997) and *Ae Fond Kiss* (2004). Anxieties about processes of de-industrialisation connect the 'underclass' dramas of Ken Loach with the naturalistic films of the Belgium-based Dardenne brothers, whilst the affect-less protagonists of *Young Adam* and *Morvern Callar* invite comparison with the dislocated, disturbed characters in the films of Gaspar Noé and Michael Haneke.

The theme of 'movement across borders' may well be a key narrative trope of recent European cinema, but many filmmakers have been faced with the practical dilemma of how (and indeed whether) to inflect subject matter of regional specificity with international appeal. Luck plays a role here, to a certain extent. Somewhat against the odds, British success stories such as *The Full Monty*, *Billy Elliot* and *Bend It Like Beckham* (2002) have struck a nerve globally, despite their parochial references and origin. Then again, the universal appeal of their narratives of unexpected triumph and generational conflict transcend their immediate contexts of post-industrial emasculation and East/West culture clash, which are pertinent concerns within contemporary British culture, although obviously not exclusively.

British film culture also retains its ties to the continent through the practical business of co-production, which is very often a determinant of casting, setting and filming locations. For example, Christopher Smith's horror film *Creep*, set almost entirely in the bowels of the London Underground system, was a German and British co-production, backed by the UK Film Council's Premiere Fund and Filmstiftung Nordrhein-Westfalen (NRW). Unsurprisingly, the central character is played by an internationally recognisable German actress – Franka Potente, the star of *Lola rennt* (*Run Lola Run*, 1998) – and the film was shot in both the UK and Germany. Production arrangements can often shed light on anomalous casting or ostensibly arbitrary plot decisions, such as the visit by the football team in *Bend It Like Beckham* to Hamburg (replete with scenes reminiscent of a travelogue), which can be explained by the film's status as a co-production between the UK, US and Germany.

The spectre of the 'Europudding' – the complicatedly co-produced project where cultural differences are not explored but homogenised to the point of blandness, incoherence or unintentional comedy (see Tookey 1995) – still hovers over transnational genre films such as *Unleashed* (2005), a vehicle scripted by Luc Besson for the Chinese martial arts star Jet Li that, despite being set in Glasgow, features hardly any Scottish accents. However, some more fruitful cross-European ties have been formed, the most prominent being those between northern British and Scandinavian film culture.

In addition to the remake of the Danish film *Den Eneste Ene* (1999) as the Newcastle-set *The One and Only* (2002), and the co-production arrangements made between Scottish and Danish companies, there has also been an interchange of creative talent. The Danish director Lone Scherfig shot the Glasgow-set *Wilbur Wants to Kill Himself* (2002) on location in Scotland and in the Zentropa studios in Denmark. Her film is a quirky tale about a young teacher's (Jamie Sives) dedication to ending his life, its fanciful depiction of the Scottish city almost on a par with that found in *Unleashed*. Andrea Arnold's *Red Road* (2006), set in the same city, was the first film to emerge out of the Advance Party project, which involved characters created by Scherfig and Anders Thomas Jensen being re-used in the work of different filmmakers. The project was overseen by Lars von Trier, whose own Scottish-set *Breaking the Waves* (1996) had borne many of the aesthetic traits demanded by the infamous Dogme 95 movement, of which von Trier was a key player.

The bonds between Danish and Scottish culture are not immediately obvious, other than their shared position of marginality in Old Europe, and a certain mordancy of humour (on the evidence of these films at least). More pragmatically, producers of Scottish cinema have located in Danish film culture a model for how a small national cinema can punch above its relative weight through a prominent strategy of creative restraints; the initial films made under the Dogme 95 banner were low-budget and formally challenging, but gained domestic and international prominence through the infamous Vow of Chastity signed by von Trier *et al*. The Dogme movement itself only had limited impact on British film culture, perhaps because an aesthetic of low-budget naturalism was already deep-rooted; the first Dogme-approved British film, the Margate-set *Gypo*, did not appear until 2005.

National and transnational cinema

In film scholarship of recent years there has been a gradual shift from an understanding of cinema in terms of national identity to an acknowledgement of the conceptual value of the transnational. Partly a recognition of the complexities of onscreen representations, this has also been a response to the increasingly globalised nature of the film industry itself, with its new conditions of financing, production and reception. Generally speaking, transnationalism is a means of addressing the ways in which people and institutions across nations are globally connected, and why the concept of the autonomous nation might be redundant.

A useful overview of this important new paradigm is offered by Elizabeth Ezra and Terry Rowden:

> Key to transnationalism is the recognition of the decline of national sovereignty as a regulatory force in global coexistence. The impossibility of assigning a fixed national identity to much cinema reflects the dissolution of any stable connection between a film's place of production and/or setting and the nationality of its makers and performers. (2006: 1)

In many respects, transnational cinema is far from new. International personnel have been involved in Hollywood since its inception, and there is a long history of co-productions. However, the 'global circulation of money, commodities, information and human beings' is indicative of an 'increasingly interconnected world-system' (ibid.).

Such is the mounting interest in the idea of national, transnational and indeed postnational cinemas – the various terms existing dialectically rather than oppositionally, as the transnational and postnational presuppose the notion of the national – that a number of related terms have come to dominate contemporary film theory. As Mette Hjort and Scott MacKenzie note:

> ...the influential critical vocabulary associated with deconstruction and psychoanalytic semiology must compete with a new set of terms: 'hybridity', 'multiculturalism', 'transnationalism', 'internationalism', 'globalisation', 'cosmopolitanism', 'exile', 'postcolonialism', to mention but some of the salient terms. (2000: 1)

Films with narratives that involve hazardous cross-national journeys – such as *In this World*, *The Road to Guantánamo*, *Last Resort* (2000) and *Tickets* (2005) – are especially amenable to this type of critical approach, as they make explicit the dislocation and processes of psychological adjustment that are central to the diasporic experience. Examples can also be located across British cinema of a phenomenon that Hamid Naficy (2001) terms 'accented cinema'. Naficy draws attention to thematic commonalities across work by exilic or otherwise displaced filmmakers, and suggests how their films are part of a conversation with host or home cultures. In recent British cinema by or about second-generation immigrants – such as *East is East* and *Bend It Like Beckham* – this typically finds expression through a thematic tension between the attractions and constraints of life in the adopted country. British cinema has also demonstrated a willingness, in films such as *The Last King of Scotland*, *Wah-Wah* (2005), *The Wind That Shakes the Barley* (2006) and *Elizabeth: The Golden Age*, to engage with the legacy of empire, a pertinent concern for scholars of post-colonial approaches to film, literature and history.

The outsider's perspective

Since the beginnings of British cinema the traffic of filmmakers departing from and arriving to the UK has been broadly equivalent. Contemporary British film culture is no different, with some directors relocating on a temporary basis (for example, Woody Allen, David Cronenberg, Lone Scherfig, Jasmin Dizdar, Rose Troche, Ronny Yu, Alfonso Cuarón, Juan Carlos Fresnadillo, Khalid El Hagar, Mira Nair) and others settling more permanently (such as the Polish-born Pawel Pawlikowski). Although it may be stretching the category of diasporic cinema too widely to include all British-set films by international directors, there is nonetheless an interesting body of work by non-UK filmmakers who convey their alien perspectives on British society and culture through visual style or the telling of insightful stories about outsiders and outcasts.

For example, Michel Blanc's London-set *Mauvais passe* (*The Escort*, 1999) provides a doubly exotic scenario. Not only is its central character – a French academic, Pierre (Daniel Auteuil), in the throes of a mid-life crisis – the kind of bourgeois figure not best served by British cinema, but his unexpected involvement in the sex industry also brings about a frankness rare in UK filmmaking, at least at the time of the film's release. Its co-writer, the novelist Hanif Kureishi, also provided the source material for Patrice Chéreau's *Intimacy* (2001), another film of (groundbreaking) sexual frankness and anomie that had more in common with trends within Gallic cinema – and, in particular, the contemporaneous vogue for 'extreme' representations of sex and sexual violence (for example, the films of Catherine Breillat and Gaspar Noé) – than any British filmmaking tradition.

Whilst a number of international filmmakers have demonstrated a keen eye for 'elements of our culture that we ourselves fail to notice' (Patterson 2007), it is the exilic work of North American directors that has perhaps been the most incisive in its excavation of British cultural identity. Examples include historically-set films such as Todd Haynes' glam-rock fantasy *Velvet Goldmine* (1998), David Mamet's *The Winslow Boy* (1999) and Robert Altman's country-house murder mystery *Gosford Park* (2001), which democratises the genre by incorporating the discontent and backstories of the lowly estate staff within its social panorama of 1930s Britain.

There has also been notable work by Woody Allen, Atom Egoyan and David Cronenberg. In Allen's thriller *Match Point* (2005), the first of his trilogy of London-set films, an aspirational Irish tennis instructor (played by Jonathan Rhys Meyers) marries into an upper-class English family and then protects his newly privileged status by murdering, in cold blood, his American lover (played by Scarlett Johansson). In *Felicia's Journey* (1999), the Canadian filmmaker Atom Egoyan, reunited with his usual cinematographer and compatriot Paul Sarossy, gives William Trevor's harrowing story of a young Irish girl Felicia (Elaine Cassidy) and her search for the father of her unborn child added chill through stark imagery of the industrial estates and suburban vistas of the English Midlands. These parts of the UK are rarely represented in British cinema, and they figure here like a buried trauma within the nation's psychic landscape. In David Cronenberg's *Spider* (2002), a schizophrenic (played by Ralph Fiennes) newly released from an institution, wanders the locations of his childhood in order to make sense of a distressing past. The fragmented worldview of the character is conveyed through an abstracted, grotesque vision of London, stripped of the chronological markers of Patrick McGrath's source novel.

The break-up of Britain?

Most critical responses to contemporary British cinema now take place within a conceptual framework that assumes the national to be fundamentally problematic and something to be dismantled, although still a force to be reckoned with (see, for example, Higson 1995; Dave 2006; Blandford 2007). Benedict Anderson's ideas about the nation as an 'imagined community' (1991) have proven to be highly influential in the distinctions that have been drawn between the 'state', with its geographical borders and political legislation, and the more fluid concept of the 'nation' as perceived through shared cultural practices, such as television, newspapers and cinema. The extent to which British cinema contributes towards or complicates this imagined community is more than ever under the spotlight.

It may seem faintly paradoxical that critical engagement with British cinema has never been greater at a moment when contestation of the national is also at its height. However, as Steve Blandford argues, it is precisely the ways in which British film (and theatre) reflects and contributes to a conversation about the meaningfulness of British identity that renders it worthy of scrutiny:

> For Britain, at this particular historical moment, it is arguably a category of more use than ever in that the tensions that have always been inherent in the idea of any kind of British national cinema have been highlighted and exposed, particularly by devolution, but also by the intensification of the other factors implicated in the 'break-up' of the idea of Britain. (2007: 15)

Even if a cohesive idea of Britain has always been dubious, questions about British identity have been pushed firmly into the popular imagination over the last two decades; manifestations of this include bestselling books on the subject like Jeremy Paxman's *The English* (1999) and the vogue for television series such as *Who Do You Think You Are?* (2004–), in which celebrities trace their ancestry.

Furthermore, the election of the Labour Party, with its commitment to regional devolution, gave fresh impetus to debates about the distinctiveness of national identity and culture, and the unity of the UK. In 1999, following a series of referendums, power was devolved from central government to the Scottish Parliament, the National Assembly for Wales and the Northern Ireland Assembly. However, plans for regional devolution in England were rejected following a negative response to a referendum in the North East in 2004. The publication of a number of books and articles on the film cultures of Wales, Scotland and Northern Ireland in recent times can be partly identified as a locally-specific response to the cultural enquiries of postcolonial theory. Other factors implicated in the 'break-up' of Britain, or at least an idea of it, include the expansion of the European Union and the influx of economic migrants from Eastern Europe, a fluctuating political relationship with Europe and the US, and an acknowledgement of ethnic and cultural diversity that has found bold new expression through second and third generations of immigrant families.

Whilst the existence of a truly 'British' cinema – however that is understood – has always been in doubt, there is agreement that the cinema's relationship to Britishness has undergone considerable change. As noted by John Hill (2001), the 'paradigm' of British national cinema is often said to have been the time of World War Two, when films such as *In Which We Serve* (1942) celebrated the elements of 'national' character that supposedly bound together the community. Although some have lamented the loss of a cinema that mirrors and promotes a unified cultural identity, others have drawn attention to the narrow definition of the 'national' in these films (synonymous with Englishness, in the main) and welcomed the 'growth of films prepared to engage with a more diverse and complex sense of national, regional, ethnic, social and sexual identities within the UK' (Hill 2001: 33). Furthermore, contemporary British filmmaking illustrates how the definition of British cinema should be replaced by an acknowledgement of the differing kinds of British *cinemas* aimed at different audiences, 'addressing different aspects of contemporary social and cultural life' and, above all, providing contrary versions of 'Britishness' (ibid.).

Cities, landscapes and journeys

In line with a budding trend within film studies of late, scholars of British film culture have been attentive to the handling of space and place in British cinema. Scrutiny has been given to the cinematic representation of cities and landscapes, and the way in which filmmakers and characters have negotiated or travelled through them. There has been particular focus on the rendering and re-imagining of specific cities and countries. As Gibson (2003), Brundson (2007) and others have acknowledged, the city of London has been portrayed with a variation that matches the multiplicity of contemporary genres, but rarely without precedent. The enchanted city of the 1990s romantic comedy is as tourist-friendly as the breezy 'Swinging London' films of the 1960s, whilst the unsettling depictions of the capital in the likes of *28 Days Later*, *Creep* and *Children of Men* (2006) follow a line of horror and post-apocalyptic fantasy. Gritty accounts of inner-city life such as *Bullet Boy* (2004) and *The Plague* (2006) are only the latest contributions to the British social realist tradition, albeit one that has traditionally been more interested in the industrial north.

However, as noted by Pamela Church Gibson, the city of London presents various difficulties for the filmmaker, not least the problem of how to relocate 'the many cinematic genres that originated in the traditions of different countries and cultures' within the 'sprawling, amorphous geography of contemporary London' (2003: 363). Whilst those who have tried to film London in 'different, demanding, innovative ways' (2003: 369) have struggled for funding and recognition, the majority settle for depicting 'different fantasy Londons' (2003: 363).

Still, contemporary British cinema has brought forth at least two innovative approaches to the representation of the capital city. In its depiction of a nocturnal underworld of asylum seekers and economic migrants propping up the tourist and business economies, *Dirty Pretty Things* compares with other films like *Beautiful People* and *The Lost Son* (1999) that also present London as a transitional, mediatory zone for those merely passing through. The second significant development is artistic, rather than political, and comes through the influence of writers such as Ian Sinclair, J. G. Ballard, Peter Ackroyd and the graphic novelist Alan Moore, who have been recognised as sharing a commitment to the exploration of urban landscape, past and present. This 'psycho-geographical' investigation of a London haunted by its literary and political inheritance connects the experimental films of Keiller and Petit/Sinclair with the Hollywood adaptations of Moore's *From Hell* (2001) and *V for Vendetta* (2005) and occult horror such as *Puritan* (2005).

As might be expected, London looms large in the depiction of the British urban experience, but recent filmmaking has been diverse in its portrayal of regional towns and cities. As ever, though, the cities of the industrial north and Scotland are more prominent than those of the south or the Midlands, despite the relatively high population of cities such as Birmingham, Leicester and Coventry. The number of films set in Liverpool, Newcastle upon Tyne and Glasgow in particular would seem to suggest that filmmakers have taken creative inspiration from cities that are models of post-industrial transformation, as well as iconic in landscape and landmarks.

British cinema's focus on urban experience hardly makes it exceptional. All the same, the scarcity of films concerned with the contemporary realities of rural life is still startling, given the UK media's prominent coverage of the fox-hunting debate, the campaigns of the Countryside Alliance and the devastating impact of outbreaks of BSE, foot-and-mouth disease and 'bird flu' on the agricultural and tourist economies. Set in North Yorkshire, *The Darkest Light* is a rare and prophetic exception. With its narrative making associations between a boy's death from leukaemia, the superstitious reaction of the local people to his sister's vision of the Virgin Mary and the spread of infection from their family's farm, the film encapsulates effectively the forebodings of rural communities of the time (as well as anticipating the 2001 foot-and-mouth epidemic).

Elsewhere, whimsical dramas like the Scottish-set *The Match* (1999) and *The Rocket Post* (2004) hark back to the communal and 'fish-out-of-water' narratives of *Whisky Galore* (1949) and *Local Hero* (1983). They peddle the kind of nostalgia astutely parodied in *Hot Fuzz*, arguably one of British cinema's most trenchant statements on how the British both ridicule and sentimentalise the parochial. Otherwise, aside from Andrew Kötting's *This Filthy Earth*, in which rustic Yorkshire is expressed as a phantasmagorical nightmare of dirt and bodily secretions, the countryside usually figures within recent filmmaking – as it always has done – as a place of either refuge or violation for the city resident. Evidently, the rural is still perceived ambivalently within the British imagination as a place of both nostalgia and dread. Despite being parodied in *Trainspotting* as a cliché of the urban film, the escapist flight to the country by weary city dwellers remains a stock scenario of British cinema. The countryside is usually depicted as place for masculine bonding, a bolt-hole from the repressive city, a site of childhood longing or a bucolic playground for the landed gentry. In the case of both the 'zombie' film *28 Days Later* and *The Queen*, in which the monarch flees to her Balmoral Estate, the countryside also provides refuge from an enraged public.

These evocations of sanctuary and prestige find counterpoint in the manifold films in which the rural becomes the site of a terrifying ordeal for the unwitting visitor. For example, in *The Low Down* (2000), a trip out of London for two young men leads to humiliation in a country pub, whereas horror films and vigilante dramas like *Straw Dogs* (1971) and *The Wicker Man* (1973) are obvious reference points for modern equivalents such as *The Last Great Wilderness* (2002), *Straightheads* (2007) and *Eden Lake* (2008). In *The War Zone* (1998) and *Enduring Love* (2004), the countryside is also the place where violatory, transgressive relationships are enacted or established.

The conspicuously high proportion of contemporary British films featuring the seaside is a clear sign of its privileged place within the nation's cultural imagination. Across many films, seaside settings or imagery of watery borders are used to express the psychological state of the grieving or traumatised – as in *The Lawless Heart* (2001), *Gabriel and Me* (2001), *Frozen* (2005), *On a Clear Day* (2005), *London to Brighton* (2006) – or the sexual experimentation of adolescents and young people (*Top Spot*).

However, coastal locations have increasingly been posited as liminal zones where cultural identity is negotiated or challenged. The seaside resort has often been presented in British cinema as a place of tawdry leisure or adolescent lawlessness but it now stands as a symbol of eroded Britishness. The availability of cheap foreign holidays has long led British holiday-makers to bypass traditional seaside resorts like Margate, Blackpool and Torquay for sunnier climes like Ibiza and Spain, as exemplified by films such as *Kevin & Perry Go Large* (2000), *It's All Gone Pete Tong* (2004) and *Morvern Callar*. In *Last Orders* (2001) and *Venus* (2006), chilly out-of-season resorts become the natural resting point for old men who have been rendered anachronistic and unclear of their legacy, and the Torquay-set *Blackball* (2003) draws comedy from a young man's disruption of the genteel world of lawn bowls.

Whilst the British seaside is frequently connoted as a place of doubtful refuge for those escaping the city or their personal demons, it has also been acknowledged as a precarious threshold for those seeking entry to the UK. In films such as *Last Resort*, *Ghosts*, *Gypo* and Penny Woolcock's *Exodus* (2007), a coastal setting is the backdrop for a contemplation of immigration and its destabilising of the social fabric. In *Last Resort*, a Russian woman and her child are interned in a nightmarishly bleak

Margate (rechristened as 'Stonehaven'), and *Ghosts* dramatises the real-life story of a group of Chinese cockle-pickers drowned in Morecambe Bay. In *Gypo* and *Ladies in Lavender* (2004), the arrival of 'foreign' bodies upon the shore unleashes sexual and familial tensions. This context gives even greater resonance, and ambiguity, to the concluding sequence of *This is England*; having dallied with far-right extremists demanding repatriation for immigrants, the young central character tosses a crumpled Union Jack flag into the sea.

These films about immigration are part of British cinema's growing attachment to stories of travel and displacement. Not just found in films about political or personal asylum, cross-country travel has now become a characteristic element of British cinema, from the epic canine voyage home in *Lassie* (2005) to the picaresque journey of wifely reclamation undertaken in the downbeat road movie *Heartlands*. Furthermore, a number of recent films have registered the wider political and cultural recognition that the nation's borders are far from impregnable, using narrative and editing strategies to efface national boundaries. A father's plan to swim the English Channel in *On a Clear Day* is actually a way of coming to terms with his son's death, but it is nevertheless symptomatic of an empathetic 'reaching out' that is also suggested in films such as *Kiss of Life, Beautiful People* and *9 Songs* (2004). Although chiefly set in the UK, these films are interspersed with sequences set elsewhere, suggesting a kind of imaginative fluidity between cultures. For example, in *Beautiful People* a racist hooligan wakes up to find himself in a Balkan war zone, and is humanised and matured by the experience.

A responsive cinema?

Traditionally slower on the uptake than other art forms with fewer industrial obstacles to immediacy, British cinema is not renowned for its swift response to social and cultural change. Furthermore, in spite of being a generator of fashion and musical trends for fifty years, with a few rare exceptions British cinema has always seemed behind the times in its promotion of home-grown pop culture, although willing to 'take advatange of Britain's significant heritage in terms of pop music' (Donnelly 2007: 117). Films and documentaries about dead icons or long-defunct bands of the 1960s and 1970s are plentiful, and include *The Filth and the Fury* (2000),

Stoned (2005), *Control* (2007) and *Joe Strummer: The Future is Unwritten* (2007), whereas *Spice World* (1997), *S Club: Seeing Double* (2003) and *I'll Be There* (2003) have provided vehicles for manufactured pop artists. But the representation of emergent youth culture tends to be rarer; the most notable exceptions being a cluster of films about clubland culture –such as *Underground* (1998), *Human Traffic* (1999) and *Sorted* (2002) – and a run of London-based dramas trading upon their 'urban' credentials (see chapter 4).

The greater willingness on the part of some filmmakers to confront issues of immigration, economic migration, surveillance culture, foreign policy, environmental concerns and extremist attitudes towards religion and nationalism can to some extent be understood as a continuation of British cinema's long-held commitment to representational extension, particularly in films in the social realist tradition. To suggest that international developments have galvanised British cinema of late into tackling subject matter of contemporaneous relevance would therefore be slightly misleading. However, the speedy arrival of drama-documentaries about very recent events – such as *United 93*, *Ghosts* and *The Road to Guantánamo* – indicates a mounting desire to deal with topics of political urgency, whilst the melodramatic thriller *The Constant Gardener* (2005) contemplated the role of the British establishment in the exploitation of the developing world by drug companies.

Despite this, contemporary British cinema tends to be reluctant to engage in any direct critique of governmental policy. Whilst there are examples of films that stoke anxieties about, for example, the education system, as *Kidulthood* (2006) does, or the infringement of civil liberties in 'fortress Britain' (*Last Resort*, *Outlaw*), these films seem wary of apportioning blame to the political figures or ideologies deemed responsible. The disillusionment expressed in youth films such as *The Plague*, where a teenager asks another to stop being 'political', or *South West Nine* (2001), which incorporates some anti-globalisation rhetoric, is more common. Compared with the rabidly anti-government films of the Thatcher years, the cinema of the Blair era is markedly less political in tenor. Furthermore, the trend for films set during the 1980s, which include *AKA*, *Billy Elliot*, *This is England*, *The Business* (2005) and *The History Boys* (2006), would suggest a film culture that is more comfortable assessing the legacy of preceding political ideologies than attending to those of the present.

The foreign policies of the Blair and Bush administrations which led to the involvement of UK and US troops in military campaigns in Iraq and Afghanistan are widely acknowledged as politically disastrous. But with the exception of the television film *The Mark of Cain* (2007), which dealt with the torture of Iraqi prisoners, the immediate response of British filmmakers to these momentous events was mostly oblique. Historically-set films like *This is England* and *Elizabeth: The Golden Age* offer vague contemporary resonances in their stories, respectively, of a boy in the 1980s becoming seduced by right-wing extremism in a time of war (the Falklands conflict), and the genesis of a 'holy war' against the Spanish. The contemporary-set *The Great Ecstasy of Robert Carmichael* (2005) culminates with a horrific act of domestic invasion and sexual violence carried out by a boy seen earlier slumped in front of television reports about the 'war on terror' and becoming aggressive on a 'media studies' field trip; a final montage of war-related imagery draws a loose parallel between the activities of Robert (Daniel Spencer) and UK foreign policy, but the film's position on the mediation of violence is unclear.

The most explicit anti-war statements have been made by the director Ken Loach, a prominent figure in campaigns such as the Stop the War Coalition. Once again, though, his stance emerges through historical parallel. *The Wind That Shakes the Barley*, his film about the origins of the republican movement in Ireland, was widely interpreted as a commentary on more recent colonial aggression. Loach's contribution to *11'09"01 – September 11* (2002), an anthology of filmic responses to the events of 11 September 2001 also used a past event, this time the overthrow of the democratically elected government in Chile (which happened, coincidentally, on 11 September 1973) to demonstrate, in the words of George W. Bush, how 'the enemies of freedom have committed an act of war on our country'. According to Loach's controversial film, the 'enemies of freedom' in Chile were inspired and subsidised by the US government itself.

It would seem that subject material with contemporary political relevance has mostly been chosen for the dramatic potential it holds. *Red Road* and *Outlaw* deal with anxieties about lawlessness and surveillance culture, but in the service of a revenge narrative. Similarly, Steven Knight, the screenwriter of the underclass thriller *Dirty Pretty Things*, claims that his story about multicultural London was necessary 'because it is where

Foregrounding the minutiae of human interaction: Nathalie Press and Emily Blunt in *My Summer of Love*

the action is, not simply to show a white middle-class audience how awful it must be to wash dishes and shine shoes' (Knight 2002).

However, this recognition that there are pressing stories to be told about British society and its place in the international community is countered by an opposing trend for films that instead foreground the minutiae of human interaction. Pawel Pawlikowski's *My Summer of Love* is typical of this 'intimist' inclination, stripping away the precise historical and political references of its source novel so as to place its intense adolescent relationship within a 'timeless, self-contained world' (Kelly 2004: 38). The poetic filmmaking of Pawlikowski, Lynne Ramsay, Andrea Arnold and others is symptomatic of this postmodern rejection of the 'metanarrative', telling stories not through classical narrative structures but through 'capturing moments like lightning in a bottle' (ibid). In a 2004 interview, Pawlikowski commented that he was drawn to filming in England because it is a 'spiritual vacuum', devoid of religious and family structures, with 'no collective belief system to measure the individual against' (in Thompson 2004: 38). He goes on to pose the question: 'What do you make films about now that people are so passionless and there are no big narratives?' (ibid.). In 2007, the director Stephen Frears made a similar point when he told an interviewer that 'we don't have big subjects now to make films about' (in Brooks 2007).

British cinema and television

British cinema and television have been mutually dependent for some time, bound together through the filmmaking divisions of the major channels, but also through a shared pool of creative talent. However, British television's commitment to public service broadcasting and its considerable reputation for comedies, dramas and documentaries, continues to have implications for the development and reception of the national cinema.

Feature-length spin-offs from popular comedy programmes and vehicles for established television performers are much less pivotal to British film culture than they were in the 1970s, when they kept a struggling industry from the brink of collapse, but films such as *Guest House Paradiso* (1999), *Ali G Indahouse* (2002), *Sex Lives of the Potato Men* (2004), *Dirty Sanchez: The Movie* (2006), *Alien Autopsy* (2006) and *Magicians* (2007) tend to be viewed as cynical, unambitious projects for undemanding multiplex or home audiences. The more impressive adaptations, like *The League of Gentlemen's Apocalypse* (2005), *Borat: Cultural Learnings of America for Make Benefit Glorious Nation of Kazakhstan* (2006) and *Mr Bean's Holiday*, have deployed the customary format of taking familiar characters beyond their natural habitat, but in a manner that is formally interesting or cinematically literate.

However, the national film culture has benefited from the continuing robustness of live and televisual comedy, which has historically given apprenticeship to the creative personnel at the forefront of comedic experimentation, such as Richard Curtis, the co-creator of *Blackadder* (1983–99) and *Mr Bean* (1990–95) and the collaborative team of Simon Pegg and Edgar Wright, whose sitcom *Spaced* (1999–2001) provided the template for the immensely successful parodies *Shaun of the Dead* and *Hot Fuzz*. A recent trend for blackly comic sitcoms – such as *The Book Group* (2002–03) and *Nighty Night* (2004–05) – has been paralleled by films like *One For the Road* (2003) and *Festival* (2005) that draw from the same well of gallows humour.

One of British television's greatest strengths is its tradition of issue-led dramas, and in terms of budget, personnel and aesthetic ambition, there is little to distinguish recent examples such as *Yasmin* (2004) and *The Government Inspector* (2005) from many films granted a theatrical release. Furthermore, politically sensitive material by directors like Ken Loach, Michael Winterbottom and Stephen Frears has been aired directly on television. Ranked alongside such formally inventive, generically pro-gressive and culturally responsive series as *Tipping the Velvet* (2002), *Shameless* (2004–), *Bleak House* (2005), *Doctor Who* (2005–) and *Life on Mars* (2006–07), these have the cumulative effect of making the national cinema appear rather less vital in comparison.

The various platforms available on British television for factual or polemical programmes has tended to restrict the theatrical release of British documentaries, other than those relating to sporting or musical subjects. British television continues to be at the forefront of experimentation with documentary formats, from the evolution of observational sitcoms like *The Royle Family* (1998–) and *The Office* (2001–03) to the *faux* documentaries of Alison Jackson. Whilst the deconstruction of documentary devices is a standard feature of much British avant-garde cinema, a little of this formal exploration has found its way into mainstream films: to comic ends in the spoof docu-dramas *The Calcium Kid*, *Mike Bassett: England Manager* (2001), *Confetti* (2006) and *Rabbit Fever* (2006); to political ends in *South West Nine*, which integrates real footage of riots into its story of contempo-rary Brixton; and to aesthetically disorientating effect in the mock 'rocku-mentary' *Brothers of the Head* (2005).

It is this tradition of experimentation that has inspired filmmakers such as Nick Broomfield, Paul Greengrass, Kevin Macdonald and James Marsh to explore and enhance the storytelling possibilities of the documentary form. Drawing upon his background in factual programming, Greengrass uses 'fly on the wall' strategies (naturalistic dialogue, handheld camera and so on) to authenticate his dramatisations of the emotive historical events of *Bloody Sunday* (2002), *Omagh* (2004) and *United 93,* the first theatrically released film about the events of 11 September 2001. Following an early career in documentary profiles, Macdonald has infused his recrea-tions of real events in *One Day in September* (1999) and *Touching the Void* (2003) with the dramatic and visual richness of popular genre filmmaking.

British cinema and literature

British cinema's reliance upon the nation's literary and theatrical herit-age for its stories, stars and creative talent has been perceived as both a signifier of quality and as an impediment to the development of a truly cinematic culture.

Adaptations of 'classic' novels from the nineteenth and early twentieth centuries continue to be a prominent and profitable strand of British filmmaking, able to exploit their audience's cognisance of the original text or its cultural eminence. A noteworthy development in recent years has been the sidelining of English Literature's less populist writers in favour of perennial favourites such as Charles Dickens and Jane Austen, whose work offers greater scope for comic energies, upbeat romantic endings and star-friendly ensemble casting. These qualities were conspicuously absent from a late-1990s cycle of films adapted from the more fatalistic and overtly literary novelists of the canon. Within a space of only a few years there were adaptations of Thomas Hardy's *Jude* (1996), *The Woodlanders* (1997), *The Scarlet Tunic* (1998) and *The Mayor of Casterbridge*, filmed as *The Claim* (2000), Henry James' *The Portrait of a Lady* (1996), *The Wings of the Dove* (1997) and *The Golden Bowl* (2000), Joseph Conrad's *The Secret Agent* (1996) and *Amy Foster* (1997), Edith Wharton's *The House of Mirth*, Virginia Woolf's *Mrs Dalloway* (1997), George Orwell's *Keep the Aspidistra Flying* (1997) and Graham Greene's *The End of the Affair* (1999).

Whereas the majority of these novels were being adapted cinematically for the first time, in the early 2000s there was a return to material well-known to British and international audiences from previous televisual, theatrical and filmic versions from the UK and Hollywood, or from their school or college studies: these include Charles Dickens' *Nicholas Nickleby* (2002) and *Oliver Twist* (2005), William Thackeray's *Vanity Fair* (2004), Jane Austen's *Pride and Prejudice* and Evelyn Waugh's *Brideshead Revisited* (2008). Not without individual merit as re-imaginings of familiar texts for contemporary sensibilities – Roman Polanski's *Oliver Twist* and Joe Wright's *Pride and Prejudice* certainly had an authentically earthy tang – these handsomely-cast titles were nevertheless indicative of the 'mainstreaming' of the literary film towards blockbuster status. At the same time, however, there were brave attempts to bring 'un-filmable' fiction to the screen. Examples include *Christie Malry's Own Double-Entry* (2000), based on a novel by the avant-garde writer B. S. Johnson, and *A Cock and Bull Story* (2005), which used the conceit of being a film about the filming of a version of *Tristram Shandy* in a style that was faithful to the 'postmodern' approach of Laurence Sterne's eighteenth-century novel.

The slowdown of lesser-known adaptations was matched by a trend for films about literary figures with a high recognition factor for contemporary audiences. The personality-led biopics *Sylvia* (2003), *Finding Neverland* (2004), *Miss Potter* (2006), *Becoming Jane* (2007) and *Iris* (2001) seem constructed primarily as vehicles for the performances of US stars (in this case, Gwyneth Paltrow, Johnny Depp, Renée Zellweger and Anne Hathaway respectively) or UK stars with an international profile (in *Iris*, Kate Winslet and Judi Dench play Iris Murdoch at different ages). Following the template of *Shadowlands* (1993), and in keeping with the celebrity-fixated culture of the age, these films dwell upon the personal struggles and tragedies faced by famous writers, rather than offer self-reflexive explorations of the creative process in the fashion of *Love is the Devil*, *Shakespeare in Love* (1998) and *Pandaemonium* (2000).

Literary adaptations and biopics provide merely one example of how contemporary British cinema fashions its identity through the appropriation of other cultural forms. *Young Adam*, *About a Boy* (2002), *The Football Factory* (2004), *Angus, Thongs and Perfect Snogging* (2008) and the *Bridget Jones* films (2001; 2004) are typical examples of how filmmakers have been able to exploit the awareness of a title, or its reputation, among certain sections of the audience, whether mainstream, cult or gender/age specific. However, it is in the realm of the Hollywood blockbuster where British writers have had the most profitable impact, with J. K. Rowling's *Harry Potter* series and J. R. R. Tolkien's *Lord of the Rings* trilogy at the forefront of a child-orientated fantasy genre that also includes *Peter Pan* (2003), *MirrorMask* (2004), *The Chronicles of Narnia: The Lion, the Witch and the Wardrobe* (2005), *Charlie and the Chocolate Factory*, *The Golden Compass* and *Stardust* (2007).

The critical and commercial success of *The English Patient* (1996) accelerated the plundering of contemporary literary fiction for prestigious material with cross-over appeal and scope for sophisticated performances by actors from the UK and beyond. As with *The Remains of the Day* (1993), and later *Oscar and Lucinda* (1997), *Possession* (2002) and *Last Orders*, Anthony Minghella's film was sourced from a Booker Prize-winning novel (by Michael Ondaatje). Taken together with other films based on short-listed texts such as Ian McEwan's *Atonement*, Zoë Heller's *Notes on a Scandal* (2006) and Monica Ali's *Brick Lane* (2007), or films drawn from literary writers like Patrick McGrath, William Boyd and Julian Barnes, these make up part of the tasteful, middle-brow core of British cinema. Many of the original novels use elliptical structures and subjective (and sometimes unreliable) narration, and these are usually translated faithfully. But whereas such devices are often employed in the 'art' film for the purpose of formal experimentation or for alienating effect, they are used in the likes of *Last Orders* and *Notes on a Scandal* as a means to advance story and enrich characterisation.

British cinema and theatre

No less significant is British cinema's historical bond with stage traditions, from which it draws not just stars, writers, directors and material, but some would say a predominantly theatrical sensibility. The adaptations of 'classic' plays produced since the mid-1990s have tended to be mischievous or revisionist rather than straightforward visualisations. Examples include Oliver Parker's playful take on Oscar Wilde's *An Ideal Husband* (1999) and *The Importance of Being Earnest* (2002), and modernised versions of Thomas Middleton's *The Changeling* (1998) and *The Revengers Tragedy* (2002).

William Shakespeare's prominence within global film culture is unwavering, inspiring in recent years a range of adaptations and re-imaginings that include *Titus* (1999), *Hamlet* (2000), *Rave Macbeth* (2001), *The King is Alive* (2001), *O* (2001) and *The Merchant of Venice* (2004). Aside from *The Children's Midsummer Night's Dream* (2001), *My Kingdom* (2001) – a relocation of *King Lear* to contemporary Liverpool – and *Shakespeare in Love*, which wittily explored the origins and reach of the Shakespeare 'industry', British cinema's contribution to this project of re-booting the Bard for the twenty-first century has been disappointingly slight. Kenneth Branagh's radical reworking of *Love's Labour's Lost* (2000) as a 1930s-style musical comedy, with Broadway songs filling the gaps left by jettisoned Shakespeare text, had the misfortune of being over-shadowed by Baz Luhrmann's *Romeo + Juliet* (1996), an energetic work of hybrid daring that made Branagh's own experiments in theatrical/cinematic fusion seem pallid in comparison.

The non-centralised nature of the film industry may have obstructed the creation of a truly British star system, but the likes of Judi Dench, Ian McKellen, Michael Gambon, Maggie Smith and Helen Mirren make up an inner circle of knighted thespian talent still active (mostly) on the stage and critically applauded for bringing theatrical kudos to British and Hollywood movies. Their regal position within international film culture, which has only really happened since the late 1990s, is exacerbated by their propensity – in the case of Dench, McKellen and Mirren at least – to take on roles as British monarchs, in the process becoming ambassadors for the British heritage industry (of which cinema obviously plays a key role). The casting of Smith, McKellen and other respected British actors in the *Harry Potter* and *Lord of the Rings* films was clearly part of a stratagem to imbue these epic Hollywood-budgeted franchises with a degree of gravitas through a connecting link to the land of their genesis. However, as Nick James observes, the 'British acting elite', allowed to shine in films such as *Gosford Park* and *Last Orders*, is often underused in British films, as 'neither the character actor nor the large ensemble seems to be as much in demand' as 'beautiful young actors, usually in small casts' (2002: 17).

Of the directors who have balanced stage and film careers, most seem to approach the cinema as a slightly more elaborate form of filmed theatre, and have accordingly chosen literary or theatrical material. Nicholas Hytner made a brave attempt to open up Alan Bennett's talky, ideas-driven *The History Boys* – first performed at the National Theatre in 2004, and filmed with the original cast – with montage sequences and more naturalistic performances. However, the director displays 'no sense of framing or rhythm' (Rayns 2006: 59). For those who have seen the stage play about grammar school boys preparing for Oxbridge, *The History Boys* serves as a pleasant but literal memento. However, a more radical, Brechtian approach may have better suited Bennett's complex material. Richard Eyre, responsible for *Stage Beauty* (2004), *Iris* and *Notes on a Scandal*, also has an utterly functional style, largely devoid of visual flourish, and trusting in his central performers to carry the story.

A striking aspect of British cinema of recent years, from *Topsy-Turvy* (1999) to *Venus*, has been the concentration of films in thrall to thespian lives or endeavours. Often, as is the case with *Shakespeare in Love* and *Stage Beauty*, a theatrical setting is used microcosmically to explore themes of, for example, gender politics and cultural identity. In *Billy Elliot*, *Mrs Henderson Presents* (2005) and *These Foolish Things* (2006), the theatre is represented as a place of solace (for either performer or audience) at times of national trauma. It is also a place, according to *Lucky Break*, *Beginner's Luck* (2001) and *Festival,* where amateurs can find either literal or figurative release, a reassuring message to a film culture aware of its insignificance on the world stage. The relevance of the theatre is only occasionally questioned in British cinema, but a rare – and rather telling – example can be found in *Wah-Wah*, Richard E. Grant's autobiographical film about the end of British rule in Swaziland. As colonial power slips away, the British residents take psychological refuge in a performance of a Gilbert and Sullivan operetta, and the limiting vision of the theatrical imagination comes under the spotlight.

3   GENRE AND BRITISH CINEMA

British film culture has tended to be characterised by an ambivalent relationship to genre. For filmmakers working in the UK, an engagement with
genre has been a means both to explore and evade notions of Britishness,
and a strategy for the targeting of international as well as local audiences.
Generic templates have mostly been used or adapted for the purpose of
popular storytelling, but they have also been drawn upon by filmmakers
intent upon political or social critique, or interrogated for reasons of formal
experimentation. Some British filmmakers are renowned for working within
a particular genre (for example, Merchant-Ivory and Ken Loach), whilst
others have done their utmost to avoid categorisation, the most notable
'genre-hoppers' of recent years being Michael Winterbottom, Danny Boyle
and Stephen Frears.

As well as being a helpful way to distinguish the personality of a
national cinema, analysis of genre also provides a means of charting the
history of British film culture through the fluctuating popularity and creativity of particular kinds of stories. Although it may not seem contentious
to claim that genres such as gangster films, horror films and comedies
are as much a part of the nation's cinematic heritage as more 'respectable' forms of filmmaking like historical films and realist dramas, it is in
fact only relatively recently that these kinds of films have received close

critical scrutiny. However, the publication of a number of monographs and anthologies on the subject of popular British genres has drawn attention to the contextual significance of their representations, their relation to international trends and the problems of classification. Beyond academia, the importance given to genre in understanding British cinema was confirmed by the structuring of the BBC's seven-part documentary series on British film history (broadcast in the summer of 2007) through episodes on individual types of filmmaking.

Questions of genre

Certain questions tend to crop up in considerations of British cinema and genre. Firstly, and perhaps mostly significantly, how helpful is it to address British cinema in generic terms? Some Hollywood-centric categorisations have even suggested that British filmmaking constitutes a genre in itself. Given the diversity of British filmmaking, this is obviously an unhelpful and unscholarly attitude. Yet it does at least serve to illustrate how the national output might be more easily defined through its 'otherness' in relation to dominant models of filmmaking (Hollywood production, in other words) than through its own inherent traits and features.

If the key genres of British cinema are difficult to fathom, this arises partly from the notoriously unstable and un-centralised nature of the native film industry. In her survey of British cinema, Sarah Street points out that the fragmentation of the industry is disadvantageous to the flowering of generic filmmaking:

> The vicissitudes of film production continue to ensure that British cinema remains an eclectic base. Repetition and difference have always been key features of film genres, but this dynamic process has been slowed down, particularly in recent years when most films are one-off productions without the security of a major studio's support. Companies come and go, and with them ideas and styles which, in a more stable environment, might have been developed in subsequent films. (1997: 112–13)

When examples of a specific type of filmmaking are so few and far between, it may be as fruitful to identify groups of films with commonalities of narrative, setting or purpose, or to locate cycles of similarly-themed work across generic boundaries. For example, the simultaneous arrival of a handful of upbeat films about disenfranchised men has been enough for an 'under-class comedy' phase to be identified and analysed, and there have also been waves of films about traumatised women, revenge, cross-cultural tension and theatrical or sporting endeavour that transcend generic clas-sification.

Another question is that of the correlation between genre activity and the success – whether in economic or creative terms – of a national film industry. If British film culture is sometimes known for engendering one-off successes and interesting clusters rather than sustainable genres, the proliferation of films of a particular genre is surely cause for optimism. However, as shown by the ostensible resurgence of the British horror film, an increase in productivity does not necessarily entail a coherence of style or content, nor profitability. Furthermore, the connection that tends to be made between genre filmmaking and popularity is called into question by the stark truth that many British films utterly fail to connect with a main-stream audience, despite their populist aim.

Furthermore, how might patterns of genre assist our comprehen-sion of the relationship between British and Hollywood cinema? It has been proposed that certain types of filmmaking, such as the historical drama and the romantic comedy, deploy visual, casting and perform-ance strategies that conform to an international consensus on Britain and Britishness. Other films are bent on playing Hollywood at its own game (*Billy Elliot*, for example), or narratively foreground the relation-ship between UK and US culture. There are also numerous examples of films that wring comedy or pathos from the transposition of scenarios most associated with American filmmaking to parochial British lives and landscapes. For example, the cross-country motorbike ride taken by the mild-mannered cuckold of *Heartlands* makes for a consciously humdrum take on the road movie, scored not to the customary driving rock music soundtrack but to the gentle strains of English folk music (by Kate Rusby), whilst *One for the Road* re-imagines the heist movie as a comedy of social observation along the lines of the television sitcom *The Office*, and the thoughtful coming-of-age drama *Son of Rambow* (2008) has its young characters taking inspiration from a notoriously violent US action film. Other films, like many in the horror genre, are better understood as part of a transatlantic or even international dialogue with filmmakers working in a similar field.

A final question relating to the deployment of genre concerns British cinema's oft-discussed commitment to realism, in terms of both a stylistic naturalism and a dedication to certain types of subject matter. This may well be the reason, coupled with budgetary confinements, why more fanciful types of filmmaking, like musicals and action films, have never taken root, other than in mocking (*Hot Fuzz*) or disguised form (*The Full Monty*). It would seem that the British musical – 'only an occasional occurrence' (Donnelly 2007: 117) in recent times – is only permitted when given an appropriately exotic backdrop, such as the non-white communities of *Babymother* (1998) and *Bollywood Queen* (2002), the Indian subcontinent of *Bride and Prejudice* (2004) or even the world of nineteenth-century opera of *Topsy-Turvy* and *Phantom of the Opera* (2004). And yet, with their sequences of public performance and prominent use of pop music on the soundtrack, *The Full Monty*, *Little Voice*, *Billy Elliot*, *Mrs Henderson Presents* and *Kinky Boots* do insinuate, together with 'backstage' films about pop stars such as *Spice World*, *Velvet Goldmine* and *Still Crazy* (1998), a latent desire for the revival of the British musical. Ironically, the few films that have attempted this directly – such as *Babymother*, *Julie and the Cadillacs* (1999) and *Bollywood Queen* – have been hamstrung by their awkward fusion of melodramatic and realist modes.

British cinema may have a prestigious tradition of realist drama, but it has been 'poor at mythologising the world around us' (Knight 2002), a feat achieved by Hollywood, which created iconic genres out of the experiences of agricultural labourers and the immigrants of the early twentieth century (the western and gangster film respectively). Although the British documentary realist tradition has been identified as a partial obstacle to the flowering of an imaginative cinematic culture, there have recently been parallel trends for the reworking of popular genres through realist strategies, and the energising of social realist films through the adoption of generic traits.

The remainder of this chapter looks at five broad and over-lapping areas of British cinema where filmmaking activity and critical response (or neglect) have been the most pronounced: the horror film, the gangster film, the comedy and romantic comedy, the realist film and the history and costume film.

The horror film

Since the turn of the century there has been a resurgence in the production of British horror films, albeit of varying styles, budget and quality. David Pirie has described the horror film as 'the only staple cinematic myth which Britain can properly claim as its own' (1973: 9), but this suggestion of a distinctly British strand of cinematic horror is open to question. Although the native tradition of Gothic literary fiction was a key influence upon the development of cinematic horror, this strain is mostly continued in current times by Hollywood financed and supervised films such as *From Hell* and *Sweeney Todd: the Demon Barber of Fleet Street* (2007).

Furthermore, until the international success of Hammer Studios in the 1950s, the British contribution to the horror genre had only ever been modest. Hammer horrors such as *The Curse of Frankenstein* (1957) and the imitative work they inspired were to dominate the market for almost two decades, but this achievement needs to be placed within the context of the relative stagnation of the Hollywood horror film during the period. Although some of the blockbuster successes of the 1970s – most famously, *The Omen* (1976), *Alien* (1979) and *The Shining* (1980) – had an element of British involvement, the native horror cinema was only kept from extinction by the occasional achievements of films such as *Hellraiser* (1987) and *Hardware* (1990). Tellingly, the creative talents that emerged in the 1990s with an interest in genre-based filmmaking had to sustain themselves by working outside of the UK, or beyond the radar of the mainstream film industry in Britain. A case in point is Chris Cunningham, the effects specialist whose music videos – which include Aphex Twin's 'Come to Daddy' – represent some of the most striking accomplishments of British horror in the late 1990s.

Whilst the renaissance of horror in the 2000s brought new visibility to British genre filmmaking, there has been no single keynote work on a par with, for example, *Ring* (1998), widely regarded as a cornerstone text for New Asian horror. Furthermore, the films of the new millennium occupy quite different positions on the generic spectrum, ranging from the gore-soaked 'splatter' films *Evil Aliens* (2005) and *Boy Eats Girl* (2005), to the survivalist thrillers *Creep, The Descent* (2005), *Wilderness* (2006) and *Severance* (2006), the surveillance thrillers *My Little Eye* (2002) and *Freeze-Frame* (2004), the serial killer film *Lighthouse* (2000), the supernatural and haunted house tales *Urban Ghost Story* (1998), *The Bunker* (2001), *Deathwatch* (2002), *Dog Soldiers* (2002), *Spirit Trap* (2005), *The Dark* (2005) and *Puritan*, the 'zombie' films *28 Days Later* and *28 Weeks Later*, the psychological thrillers *The Hole* (2001), *Trauma* (2004) and *Blinded* (2004), the parodies *Shaun of the Dead* and *Wallace and Gromit: The Curse of the Were-Rabbit*, the self-reflexive *Last Horror Movie* (2003), and the anthology *Cradle of Fear*.

This eclecticism may explain the limited critical and popular recognition of a 'new wave' of British horror. But another reason is that these films have had to compete in an international market now crowded with horror productions and therefore very different to the situation in the 1950s and 1960s when Hammer enjoyed their golden era.

Aside from their sheer volume, these films are perhaps most distinguishable from their 1990s counterparts through their professionalism of approach. Richard Stanley sees the 1990s as a 'decade whose only genre entries amounted to amateurish efforts, home movies and fan boy fluff too impoverished or basically incompetent to reach a wider audience' (2001: 193). Indeed, the revival of British horror is as bound up with tax breaks and technological advances as it is with a creative renaissance. Proof of the benefits of developments in computer-generated imagery (CGI) can be found in the films that emerged from the very 'fan boy' netherworld written off by Stanley; that is, the low-budget works made primarily for a cult audience. Take, for example, the gulf in technical competency between Jake West's comic splatter film *Evil Aliens* and his earlier *Razor Blade Smile* (1998), a dreary and uninvolving contemporary vampire story. Whatever one thinks of *Evil Aliens*, its inclusion of over 140 digital effects shots and its pioneering use of Sony High Definition cameras gives it a greater degree of slickness and ambition. Ultra low-budget fare such as *The Last Horror Film* and the Amicus tribute *Cradle of Fear* have a sincerity and resourcefulness that some might find endearing, but as with 'sexploitation' films like *Sacred Flesh* and *Pervirella* (1997), their rough-hewn marginality leaves them out of step with a film culture marching to the middle-ground.

To some degree, comic films such as *Shaun of the Dead*, *The League of Gentlemen's Apocalypse* and *Wallace and Gromit: Curse of the Were-Rabbit* – all affectionately magpie-like in their intertextual borrowings but also attentive to characterisation and narrative flow – represent the infiltration of a 'fan' sensibility into the mainstream. These particular films also draw their comic energies from the importation of scenarios commonly associated with either American or historically-set UK horror into the kinds of landscapes familiar from British dramas and television soap operas, such as the anonymous suburbs of the capital and the reassuring 'north' of *Coronation Street* (1960–) and *The Full Monty*. In survivalist horrors such as *Severance* and *Dog Soldiers*, a similarly disorientating effect comes via sudden and unexpected tonal changes between broad, capricious humour and brutally nasty violence (this also happens to be a feature of the contemporary gangster film).

The national cinema's gravitational pull towards realism has resulted in some horror films with a naturalistic edge that therefore have some claim to being markedly British in attitude. The 'kitchen-sink' legacy of social accuracy and observational technique surfaces in *Urban Ghost Story*, *The Last Great Wilderness*, *28 Days Later*, *Dead Man's Shoes* (2004), *Wild Country* (2005) and *Eden Lake*.

A celebrated early sequence of the 'zombie' movie *28 Days Later* depicts a young Irishman, Jim (Cillian Murphy), waking up amidst an eerily evacuated central London (created without the aid of CGI). All that remains are upturned cars and a collage of notices about missing people that is reminiscent of those seen in the aftermath of terrorist attacks. Once it becomes plain that the 'rage' virus has infected all but a small band of survivors, he heads north to Manchester for promised sanctuary. Having worked previously on Dogme films such as *Festen* (*The Celebration*, 1998) and *Julien Donkey-boy* (1999), the cinematographer Anthony Dod Mantle uses the DV format to bring a combination of handheld intimacy and expressionistic flourish to Alex Garland's thoughtful fable about the perils of genetic modification and bio-terrorism. John Murphy's haunting score, which lends an epic quality to the scenes of devastation, works in counterpoint with the visual and editing techniques familiar from docu-drama formats; the film's achievement is to defamiliarise both the genre and the landscape.

In addition to their stylistic inflection towards naturalism, a few of these horror films also provide an element of social and political commentary. Anxieties over cultures of surveillance are exploited by *My Little Eye* and *Freeze-Frame* (a theme that crops up frequently across recent British cinema, most notably in the revenge thrillers *Red Road* and *Straightheads*). With regard to the more gory films, *Dog Soldiers* and *28 Days Later* throw barbs at the US and UK military, *Creep* renders its glamorous party-girl heroine Kate (Franka Potente) indistinguishable from a beggar at the end

Social and political commentary: Kate (Franka Potente) terrorised in the London
Underground in *Creep*

of her ordeal at the hands of a victim of scientific experimentation, and
in *Severance* the butchery of members of a team-building excursion to
Eastern Europe speaks vaguely of the disposability of corporate workers.

The horror film that has invited the most rigorous allegorical scrutiny to
date is *28 Weeks Later*, not least because its depiction of central London as
a US protectorate mirrored the perception of the film itself as a Hollywood
'colonisation' of a British franchise. The brutal treatment of the contami-
nated by the US troops does indeed convey something of 'America's post-
7/7 suspicion and profound lack of sympathy for Britain and the dangerous
spores and germs being incubated on our island' (Bradshaw 2007). Having
lost control, the troops are unable to distinguish between the infected
and non-infected, leading to 'friendly fire' casualties. However, the sympathetic characterisation of some of the peace-keeping soldiers as 'good
Americans' leading the protagonists to safety complicates any reading of
the film as a critique of US foreign policy.

Although some of these films set or partially set in the capital have
made prominent use of internationally recognisable landmarks so as to
enhance marketability – for example, Big Ben and the Houses of Parliament
in *28 Days Later*, the London underground in *Creep* – the contemporary
British horror film is far less England-centred than it was previously.
However, of the films with identifiably provincial settings, many were actually filmed partially or totally in Europe. For example, Luxembourg stands
in for Scotland in *Dog Soldiers*, the Isle of Man for Wales in *The Dark* and
Germany for England in *Creep*, fundamentally for economic reasons.

Similarly, the US-set *The Descent* was made in the UK, whilst *Severance* was shot in Hungary and the Isle of Man and set in Eastern Europe.

It is debatable whether this 'Europeanisation' of the British horror film has had an impact on content, however. But the tendency (or perhaps necessity) of many of the filmmakers to uproot their productions beyond the UK is mirrored by the recurrence of stories in which individuals or groups of characters are transplanted into hostile, unfamiliar landscapes. It could also be argued that the formal reflexiveness of these films connects them to a continental tradition of exploratory horror – such as *Switchblade Romance* (2003) and *Calvaire* (2004) – but also of 'art' cinema more generally. A common occurrence is the trick ending. Effective examples include the possibility that the victorious heroine of *The Descent*, Sarah (Shauna Macdonald), may be insane (a coda removed from the US version), the revelation that the 'victim' of *The Hole* (played by Thora Birch) has actually orchestrated the events of the film, and the 'alternative' conclusions of *28 Days Later* which appear on the DVD versions of the film.

Although the increased visibility of British horror cinema in the new millennium has made it difficult to ignore, it is significant that the films with the greatest critical and cultural impact have been those with the highest levels of generic impurity. Whilst the similarly Romero-influenced *Shaun of the Dead* and *28 Days Later* benefited from their borrowings from other genres – respectively, comedy and post-apocalyptic science fiction – the British horror film still lacks critical respectability. A slightly different fate has befallen films that can be more closely identified with the science fiction genre. Although fewer in number, these have enjoyed greater prestige. This has either been because of their origins as literary or graphic fiction, as in the case of the dystopian thrillers *Children of Men* and *V for Vendetta*, or through their association with the subgenre of 'intellectual' science fiction exemplified by *2001: A Space Odyssey* (1968) and *Solaris* (1972), films which have evidently had some influence upon the philosophically-minded *Sunshine* and *Code 46*.

The gangster film

The acceleration of crime-related films that followed in the wake of the phenomenally successful *Lock, Stock and Two Smoking Barrels* (1998) was quickly recognised as a significant development, if not universally welcome. Condemned equally on moral and aesthetic grounds, these films 'jostled the delicate national cinema like muggers in an alley' (Chibnall 2001: 280). Alexander Walker denounced this crime wave, fuelled by turn-of-the-century Lottery funding opportunities, as indecent in its glee-ful and cynical brutality, noting how 'each succeeding annal of British gangster-land grew paler and more self-parodic' (2004: 306). Danny Leigh viewed the cycle as 'bourgeois pornography', given that the 'vast bulk of violent crime remains – as ever – perpetrated by and on the working class' (2000: 25).

Within British cinema, stories involving crime and the criminal under-world have never been the sole preserve of the gangster film. Indeed, realist films such as *Sweet Sixteen* (2002) and *London to Brighton* have placed a spotlight on the insidious, predatory impact of organised crime and drug trafficking upon the resident and migrant underclass, whilst the mundane realities of the criminal justice system throughout the twentieth century have been explored in the historical dramas *Another Life* (2001), *Vera Drake* (2004) and *Pierrepoint* (2005).

In her account of the films that predated the late 1990s gangster boom, Claire Monk makes the point that the movies that 'responded best to the social realities shaping 1990s crime were those that departed from traditional genre models' (1999: 173); she cites Shane Meadows' *Small Time* (1996) as a good example, for its focus on petty criminals. The films of the contemporary gangster cycle, which reached its peak around the turn of the millennium, were mostly disinterested in the inter-connections between underworld and underclass. Yet the story of desperate men being seduced into criminal activity is a common enough scenario, as found in *Small Time Obsession* (2000), *Going Off Big Time* (2000), *Out of Depth* (2000), *One Last Chance* (2004) and *One For the Road*. The increasing professionalism of the crime world is alluded to in *Layer Cake* (2004), *Dead Man's Cards* (2006) and elsewhere, but there is little in British crime cinema of equivalence to revisionist US television dramas and films like *The Sopranos* and *Analyze This* (1999), which consider the changing psyche of the gangland boss or foot-soldier as the twenty-first century approaches.

Nor are these films responsive to the economic realities shaping crime in the new millennium. The high-profile reporting of daring real-life heists (such as the attempted theft of diamonds from the Millennium Dome in

2002) and the continued fascination with gangsters like the Krays, are suggestive of the reassurance taken from 'old-fashioned' criminality in an era dominated by white-collar crime and the decidedly unglamorous business of illegal immigration and sex trafficking. Recent gangster films have also been perceived as retrograde in their cultural politics, their empty recycling of filmic references, and their indebtedness to Guy Ritchie's *Lock, Stock and Two Smoking Barrels* for style and narrative structure.

Ritchie's film is usually blamed for setting the gangster bandwagon in motion, although this is to overlook the role played by films such as Antonia Bird's *Face* (1997) and Jez Butterworth's *Mojo* (1997) in making the crime film fit for purpose in the Blair era. The history of the underworld film can be traced back to the disreputable 'spiv' films of the 1940s and 1950s, but the key reference points in the post-Ritchie cycle are the seminal works of gangster chic from the late 1960s onwards, *The Italian Job* (1969), *Performance* (1970), *Get Carter* (1971) and *The Long Good Friday* (1980). Incorporated into the mid-1990s valorisation of 'Cool Britannia' pop culture, these films also became touchstones for the 'new lad' phenomenon promoted in certain quarters of the media and typically understood as a reactionary manifestation of post-feminist anxieties.

Some commentators expressed regret that filmmakers had copied the nihilistic tone of the 'classics', but replaced their sense of moral purpose with empty recycling and a dubious amorality. But as Steve Chibnall points out, 'professional crime provides a linking motif for a spectrum of films from those that strive for unvarnished authenticity to those that cheerfully peddle myth' (2001: 282). His description of the two ends of this spectrum as 'gangster light' and 'gangster heavy' acknowledges the difference between the films where knowing pastiche is achieved through self-reflexive strategies and one-dimensional characterisations, and the films which pay attention to detail of period and place, naturalistic dialogue and psychological complexity.

According to Chibnall, Ritchie's films fall into the former category, conjuring up a 'London of the imagination, floating in time somewhere in the last thirty years without solid temporal or geographical anchors' (2001: 284). The shaggy-dog narratives of *Lock, Stock and Two Smoking Barrels* and *Snatch* unfold in a hermetically sealed world, an almost exclusively male terrain of fakery and masquerade. The cast of unlikely characters in these films include a group of cockney gangsters impersonating Orthodox Jews, a Samoan who runs an East End pub, a pair of clownish Liverpudlians, gypsies ('pikeys') who exaggerate their accent and a Russian who wears the clothes of an English aristocrat. The cast of Snatch in particular may be nationally and ethnically diverse, but the provocative characterisation produces a 'kind of paradoxical politically incorrect multiculturalism' (Dave 2006: 16). Furthermore, the casting of the ex-footballer Vinnie Jones in leading roles in Ritchie's first two feature films is indicative of a conscious courting of the 'new lad' demographic of twentysomething male soccer fans.

These qualities of exaggerated stereotyping, attacks on good taste and intertextual referencing are the hallmarks of other 'gangster light' films such as Love, Honour and Obey (2000), Circus (2000) and Rancid Aluminium (2000). A character in Love, Honour and Obey makes the observation that 'all gangsters are performers', a reference not only to Nicolas Roeg and Donald Cammell's Performance (1970), but to the creation of the film itself, which was co-devised by the participants, a gang of well-known British actors who play underworld characters partly based on themselves. Registering the recurrent conception of identity as 'performance' in these films, Paul Dave stresses that this is far removed from the 'theoretical project informing the cultural politics of difference' (2006: 17); speaking specifically of Ritchie's films, he argues that the performances are 'wearily familiar ones which produce stereotypes of Englishness and masculinity' (ibid.). This 'faux-ness', witnessed across British cinema generally, has a partial explanation in the 'politics of spin' (Chibnall 2001: 290) engendered by the New Labour government. Cora Kaplan, on the other hand, claims that the self-consciously parodic representations of working-class experience are the result of the Blairite suppression of any mention of class other than in a 'retro-social performance' (2004: 101).

At the 'heavier' end of the crime spectrum are the most dramatically satisfying gangster films, namely Paul McGuigan's Gangster No. 1 (2000), Jonathan Glazer's Sexy Beast (2000) and Paul Sarossy's Mr In-Between (2001). These use familiar narratives – such as the 'rise and fall' and the 'one last job' – as a means to explore the kind of themes found in Greek tragedy or religious parable. All three films are structured through a triangular relationship between two men and the woman who offers one of them redemption. The nameless and violently unstable character of Gangster No.1 (played at different ages by Paul Bettany and Malcolm

The rise and fall of the gangster: Gal (Ray Winstone) brought out of retirement in *Sexy Beast*

McDowell) usurps his rival's position of power, but at the expense of his own humanity. In *Sexy Beast*, a similarly psychopathic character, Don Logan (Ben Kingsley), arrives at the Spanish home of retired criminal Gal (Ray Winstone) to entice him back to the UK to take part in a heist. In *Mr In-Between* a nonchalant, autistically tidy hitman, Jon (Andrew Howard), is humanised through his relationship with a school friend's wife, Cathy (Geraldine O'Rawe), who he ultimately kills in order to save her and her child from the murderous intentions of his demonic gangland boss, the Tattooed Man (David Calder).

It is tempting to read the fates of the characters in these films as emblematic of the more recent fortunes of the gangster film. However, generic analysis is frustrated by the heterogeneity and hybridity of the films with an underworld theme.[1] Furthermore, if it is usually possible to place texts within generic cycles by way of their status as classic, revisionist or parodic, this task is made impossible by the simultaneous arrival of gangster films that displayed all these qualities, sometimes unwittingly. In *Sexy Beast*, Gal has disturbingly surreal dreams about a giant rabbit, but these visions are no less bizarre than Guy Ritchie's *Revolver* (2005), a brave attempt to bend his customary caper format in the direction of the European art film before he returned to more familiar territory in *RocknRolla* (2008), and Lab Ky Mo's *9 Dead Gay Guys* (2002), a cheeky Ritchie-style romp which gives free reign to the homoeroticism barely suppressed in most British crime cinema of the era. Time will tell whether these films represent new directions or dead ends for the British gangster film, but ten years after the release of *Lock, Stock and Two Smoking Barrels*, the cycle seemed to have lost momentum, perhaps because of the social climate – high-profile cases of gang killings have made the subject less palatable – or maybe simply because of creative exhaustion. However, like the boulder hurtling down towards the reclining Gal in *Sexy Beast*, the crime film may yet return to brutishly awaken British cinema from its slumber.

Comedy

In her brief survey of the comedy genre Susan Hayward notes that although Britain has a 'strong tradition with its Ealing Comedies and Carry On movies', these are 'past history (1940–50s and 1958–78 respectively) – as indeed is the British film industry itself' (1996: 56). There is much to contest and unpick here. Hayward's implication that popular genres such as comedy need to be supported by a stable production system has some validity, but the idea of the British comic tradition being exhausted is surely disproved by the successful wave of 'rom-coms' and comedy-dramas from the mid-1990s onwards. Furthermore, Hayward's proposal that the end of the Carry On cycle in the late 1970s signalled the demise of the British comedy tradition overlooks the contribution of filmmakers and writers such as Bill Forsyth, Willy Russell and Mike Leigh to the evolution of the regional comedy and the comedy-drama of social observation in the 1980s.

The films of the 1990s extended and refined these formats, and developed some new ones too, such as the 'urban fairy tale' (as discussed in the next section), but connections could still be made with previous traditions. In her discussion of communal comedies such as *The Full Monty*, Julia Hallam suggests that they betray a hankering for the spirit of the Ealing comedies and their projection of 'an idealised image of a nation united by adversity' (2000: 267). Certainly, Ealing ghosts re-surface whenever delight is drawn from mischievous collective endeavour, regional whimsy or the subversive energies behind a façade of propriety in films such as *House!* (2000), *Saving Grace* (2000) and *Grow Your Own* (2007). At the same time, the more disreputable tradition of vulgar comedy, as epitomised by the sex comedies and television spin-offs of the 1970s, lives on via scatological or fornication-based films like *Large* (2001), *Sex Lives of the Potato Men*, *Kevin & Perry Go Large* and *Dirty Sanchez: The Movie*, which usually leave critics in a state of either revulsion or incomprehension.[2]

Albeit broadly defined, the humorous film continues to be a significant component of British cinema, despite Hayward's assertions to the contrary. Nigel Mather proposes that one of the most distinctive aspects of British cinema in the 1990s was the successful interaction of comedy and drama 'within a group of significant and influential films' (2006: 1). Mather identifies three key strands which provide 'generically flexible and robust narrative forms': communal comedies, ethnic comedy-dramas and romantic comedies. The first category encompasses films dealing with economic and social issues, such as *Brassed Off* (1996) and *The Full Monty*, whilst the second group includes films such as *East is East* which consider the 'contrasting emotional and intellectual values of first-, second- and third-generation immigrants to Britain' (2006: 185). The romantic comedies, on the other hand, explore the 'hopes and fears of associated individuals seeking love and personal fulfilment in their private lives' (ibid.).

This encounter between the comedic and the realistic may give these cycles distinction, but it also raises questions about the effectiveness of humour in dealing with serious subject matter. By its very nature, comedy offers a challenge to realism, and comedy-dramas consequently embody the tension in British film culture between the documentary-realist impulse and the 'melodramatic' influences of literary and theatrical culture, from which the comic tradition emerges. As Hayward notes, comedy can be 'perceived as serving a useful social and psychological function in that it is an arena, or provides an arena, where repressed tensions can be released in a safe manner' (1996: 55). It can also be a space for the interrogation of ideas about cultural identity. However, in its foregrounding of stereotype, comedy can equally serve to reinforce certain prejudices pertaining to gender, sexuality, class and ethnicity. Indeed, the comedy-dramas of the 1990s and beyond have come under considerable critical scrutiny for their alleged conservatism and masculinism.

Mather's account of these films is more sympathetic. He makes the case for their role in the regeneration of British film culture in the 1990s and their continuation of earlier traditions, and extrapolates out of them a more profoundly hopeful message:

> One of the achievements of the British comedy-dramas … is that while they reveal an awareness of the tragic elements in British and Western culture they also work to celebrate the continuing

existence of the 'comic', with its attendant qualities of spirit, resilience and a belief that mankind will persevere and carry on until the very end. (2006: 194)

The question remains as to whether the contemporary-set comedy-dramas of communal activity, ethnic experience and the path towards true love are principally phenomena of the 1990s. These kinds of narratives have not disappeared altogether, but their diminishing impact has shifted them to a more peripheral position in British film culture. Later films such as *Mrs Caldicot's Cabbage War* (2000) and *Kinky Boots* (2005), which tackle, respectively, the ill treatment of the elderly in care homes and homophobia, can be more effectively categorised as late entries in the established cycles, rather than as new directions.

Romantic comedy

The significance of the romantic comedy within British film production of the 1990s is quite remarkable given the lack of precedent. Although an indigenous tradition of romance-themed films is discernible, up until the late 1990s there had hardly been any direct equivalences to the screwball comedies of the classical Hollywood era or to modern US 'chick flicks' such as *Pretty Woman* (1990). However, the international success of *Four Weddings and a Funeral* signalled that there was creative and economic mileage in a British take on a Hollywood staple.

An Anglo-American romance: Julia Roberts and Hugh Grant collide in the romantic comedy *Notting Hill*

Richard Curtis, the writer of *Four Weddings and a Funeral* and *Notting Hill*, co-writer of the *Bridget Jones* films, and writer/director of *Love Actually*, is generally regarded, in tandem with the production company Working Title, as the initiator of the British rom-com boom. Ten years after the release of *Four Weddings and a Funeral* its legacy was still visible in films about middle-class, metropolitan characters with a propensity for inventively posh swearing and mad dashes across town in pursuit of their beloved, a synopsis which neatly sums up *Imagine Me and You* (2005) but also applies, to varying degrees, to many other films that shared enough traits to be logically categorised as a (sub)genre by critics and audiences.

The Anglo-American romance of *Four Weddings and a Funeral* was replayed in its spiritual 'sequel' *Notting Hill*, as well as in *Martha, Meet Daniel, Frank and Laurence* (1998) and *Wimbledon* (2004), whilst American actresses showed off their English accents in *Sliding Doors* (1997), *The Truth About Love* (2004), the *Bridget Jones* films and *Imagine Me and You*. As discussed in chapter 2, the films which focus on developing relationships between British and American characters can be seen as symptomatic of the wider desire to 'forge closer working relationships between British and Hollywood production companies, and to demonstrate that Britain was capable of producing films with outstanding appeal to international audiences' (Mather 2006: 120).

It is tempting to overstate the significance of these films as manifestations of British unease about the imbalance of power in the 'special relationship'. Their focus on issues of compatibility, like their deployment of stereotypical secondary characters, is an attribute of the modern romantic comedy in general, rather than specific to the British variant. However, their representation of Anglo-American associations is revealing nonetheless. In the thematically-similar *Notting Hill* and *Wimbledon*, a self-confessed under-achiever becomes besotted with an American at the top of her profession, and not only wins the girl but also some of her winning streak, whilst the women – and, it is hoped, the international market – are wooed by the charms of the mother country and the authenticity of its heritage and people.

In their establishing of a contrast between brash, demonstrative American characters and self-effacing but culturally confident British characters, these films perpetuate the idea of Britishness as somehow less performative and more historically grounded. However, this is countered by the various films in which audiences are given the opportunity to assess how well non-UK actresses impersonate English characters. More of a concern for British audiences and critics, the evaluation of the 'authenticity' of accent and mannerisms actually draws attention to the constructedness of national identity. For example, in his review of *Sliding Doors*, Mark Steyn claims that 'Gwyneth Paltrow presents a far more enchanting vision of Englishness than other English actresses I can think of' (1998: 44). This 'enchantment' may partly derive from the limited signification of class when the characters are played by non-British actresses; most tend to adopt an 'estuary' English accent that is sufficiently well-heeled without being geographically specific.

For Robert Murphy, a defining feature of films of the romantic comedy cycle of the late 1990s was their fairy-tale quality.

> Fairy-tales consciously mythologise their setting and social setting and social relationships, allow coincidences and magic to determine events and structure their narratives in such a way that the protagonist of the story undergoes a series of tests or ordeals before achieving his or her goal. (2001: 293)

According to Murphy, contemporary urban romances such as *This Year's Love* (1999), *Sliding Doors, Martha, Meet Daniel, Frank and Laurence* and *Notting Hill* contain characters that conform to recognisable fairy-tale archetypes, and who dwell in a London re-imagined as an 'enchanted village [of] chance encounters and coincidental meetings' (2001: 297). In other words, to condemn these stories for their representation of a city free from social and ethnic tensions is to overlook their potency as fantasies of reassurance and unity.

Although these romantic comedies largely evoke an 'atmosphere of untroubled contentment' (Dave 2006: 46), the idyllic communities they represent are occasionally disrupted by the inequities of the world beyond. References to global tragedies are a conversational leitmotif of *Notting Hill*: there is mention of 'Third World debt', 'earthquakes in the Far East' and the 'starving in Sudan'. What is more, *Love Actually* begins with a reference to the events of 11 September 2001, *The One and Only* introduces an African orphan to a glossily-filmed Tyneside, and *Bridget Jones: The Edge of Reason* sees its heroine arrested for drug smuggling and confined to a Bangkok jail. This incursion of the 'authentically' miserable can perhaps be explained as the materialisation of the realist impulse of British cinema, but within the context of these films the references and scenarios are troubling and sometimes in dubious taste.

The realities of a culturally varied London may have been ignored in *Notting Hill*, but the romantic comedies of the 2000s have shown a greater willingness to reflect cultural and regional diversity, if to little real effect. Whereas the films of the late 1990s were predominantly London-centred, later entries to the rom-com cycle have applied visual fairy-dust to provincial cities famed for their strong local identity and their commitment to cultural regeneration projects, most notably Newcastle upon Tyne in *The One and Only*, Bristol in *The Truth About Love* and Glasgow in *Nina's Heavenly Delights* (2006). The incorporation of eye-catching landmarks – for example, the Millennium and Clifton Suspension Bridges (in Newcastle and Bristol) – gives the films a regional flavour, but the expression of the 'enchanted city' is otherwise homogenous. Similarly, the focus upon the courtship of characters of the same sex in *Imagine Me and You* and *Nina's Heavenly Delights* is theoretically progressive, but rendered innocuous by the formulaic nature of the narrative.

The limited success of these attempts to re-invigorate the increasingly jaded Curtis template with regional and sexual variation did not bode well for the future of the British romantic comedy. By 2007, the format established by *Four Weddings and a Funeral* had lost much of its creative and commercial robustness, and films such as *Heroes and Villains* (2006) that thoughtlessly rehashed the 'component body parts of a typical Working Title-style British romantic comedy' (Davies 2007: 64) were deemed superfluous and conformist. It is thus appropriate that the 'what next?' question that they pose is also a recurring narrative scenario of the twenty-first century British rom-com. Unlike the majority of the 1990s films, *The One and Only*, *The Truth About Love*, *Imagine Me and You* and *Bridget Jones: Edge of Reason* all begin with a marriage or an established partnership, and then take their dissatisfied characters in new romantic directions.

The realist film

The social realist tradition has long been recognised as a major strand of British filmmaking, although the existence of a coherent realist genre is doubtful (see Lay 2002). It is perhaps more appropriate to identify a realist impulse that continues to manifest itself through subject matter or form, or a combination of the two.

Surveying the most recent examples of films with some claim to realism, two aspects are immediately apparent. Firstly, the masculinist bias of much British social realist cinema has been challenged by a proliferation of films centring upon female characters, very often from the perspective of a female writer or director (see the discussion of the work of Lynne Ramsay and Andrea Arnold in the next chapter). A second feature is the incorporation of stylistic and narrative devices from different types of filmmaking, from traditions of art cinema to popular forms of storytelling such as the thriller and the musical. Although formal hybridity has long been a key trait of realist cinema, the dispersal of the realist tendency across an extremely broad range of films is typical of contemporary British film culture's penchant for convergence. A comparison of the creative tactics of three directors who tend to be lazily lumped together as keepers of the same realist flame – Ken Loach, Mike Leigh and Shane Meadows – reveals the multiplicity, rather than uniformity, of realist strategies available to the contemporary filmmaker.

In a career spanning over forty years, Ken Loach has been an unwavering chronicler of the dispossessed and an advocate for an unfussy, quasi-documentary approach that strives for naturalism in performance and situation. The tragi-comic tone of some of Loach's films of the 1990s, particularly *Riff Raff* (1990) and *Raining Stones* (1993), was adopted by some of the most successful British films of the decade. But unlike the upbeat *Billy Elliot* and *The Full Monty*, Loach's plots are characterised by a fatalistic drive towards a grim denouement. *My Name is Joe* (1998), *The Navigators* (2001), *Sweet Sixteen* and *The Wind That Shakes the Barley* all conclude with the death of a significant character, and the despair of the central protagonists. The US-set *Bread and Roses* and the historical film *The Wind That Shakes the Barley* continue a strand of Loach's work – stretching back through *Land and Freedom* (1995) to his television series *Days of Hope* (1975) – in which relevant political lessons are drawn from struggles taking place beyond contemporary Britain.

The involvement of the screenwriter Paul Laverty in almost all of Loach's features since *Carla's Song* (1996) contributes to the consistency of purpose in his recent films – and brings a geographical focus too, as three of them are set in Glasgow – but Loach's oeuvre has been more varied than his detractors would admit. The cross-cultural romance of *Ae Fond Kiss* takes place between young professionals rather than the Glaswegian underclass, and *It's a Free World...* (2007) dares its audience to sympathise with a young woman who is complicit in the exploitation of economic migrants.

In a similar fashion, Mike Leigh's popular reputation as a comic satirist of suburban despair is derived as much from his film and television work of the 1970s to the early 1990s – such as *Bleak Moments* (1971), *Abigail's Party* (1977) and *Life is Sweet* (1990) – as from his later work, which offers both continuities and points of departure, most notably the telling of stories set wholly or partly in the past. Leigh's famous creative method of improvisatory workshops with ensemble casts tends to result in domestic dramas about fissures in family relationships that are ultimately either repaired or fractured forever. In the gloomy council-estate drama *All or Nothing* (2002), the heart attack of a churlish, overweight teenager, Rory (James Corden), triggers a reconciliation reminiscent of that which concludes the similarly-themed *Secrets and Lies* (1996), but in *Vera Drake*, the revelation of the involvement of a mother (Imelda Staunton) in illegal abortions destroys the unity of a close-knit working-class family of the 1950s.

Two characteristic features of Leigh's earlier work, an emphasis upon class friction and a tendency towards caricature, are much less prominent in his Blair-era films, and are replaced in *Career Girls* (1997) and *Topsy-Turvy* by a self-conscious exploration of his own creative methods and preoccupations. In *Career Girls*, two college flatmates (played by Katrin Cartlidge and Lynda Steadman) who made up a makeshift family unit reunite as late twenty-somethings. As if in acknowledgement of the criticisms of his broader earlier work, Leigh invites the viewer to compare the excessively mannered performances and *mise-en-scène* of the 'flashback' sequences with the comparatively naturalistic modern-day scenes. The multi-layered *Topsy-Turvy* locates a parallel for the complicated genesis of the director's own collaborative projects in the story of the evolution and premiere of the late-nineteenth-century comic operetta *The Mikado* (1895) by Gilbert and Sullivan. The D'Oyly Carte ensemble is yet another of Leigh's dysfunctional families overcoming private crises for a public display of harmony. The unlikely and awkward partnership between the cosmopolitan composer Sullivan (Allan Corduner) and the parochial satirist Gilbert (Jim Broadbent) is suggestive of the tension between experimentation and conformity in Leigh's work, and British film culture in general. *Topsy-*

Turvy also addresses the impossibility of the realist filmmaker's quest for verisimilitude through its account of the production of *The Mikado*, which is acknowledged as a simplistic, even racist account of Japanese culture, despite the attempts of its creators to incorporate a degree of authenticity in costume and performance. At the same time, just as the exotic setting of *The Mikado* enabled its creators to sharpen their mockery of Victorian England, so Leigh and fellow filmmakers have used historical settings as a vehicle for contemporary concerns.

Allusions to Leigh and Loach occur with wearying frequency in reviews of films that document lives on the fringes of society in a naturalistic or comic fashion. Yet the influence of Loach can certainly be felt in stories about working-class characters driven inexorably towards tragedy, such as *A Way of Life* and *Bullet Boy*, and Leigh's 'chamber' comedies are a reference point for satirical ensemble dramas like *Chunky Monkey* (2001) and *Confetti*. The 'slice of life' tradition of loosely-plotted, finely-observed naturalism has been maintained by the youth dramas *Underground* and *The Plague*, films that lead towards dramatic conclusions but are unafraid to linger on the inconsequential business of teenage courtship, musical performance, tea-making and small talk.

However, it is the Midlands-born Shane Meadows who is arguably the most influential realist British filmmaker of the era. An auteur in the sense that his films are mostly set around his place of birth, are often concerned with the relationship between male authority figures and their vulnerable charges, and have a consistent tone of blackly comic naturalism, Meadows' work is also distinguished by a liberal approach to genre, taking inspiration from the sporting film in *Twenty Four Seven* (1997), the revenge thriller in *Dead Man's Shoes*, the western in *Once Upon a Time in the Midlands* (2002) and the coming-of-age drama in *A Room for Romeo Brass* (1999), *This is England* and *Somers Town* (2008). In general, Meadows has used generic references not in the service of empty pastiche but as a framework for the consideration of social issues of pressing concern in contemporary Britain: the bullying of vulnerable teenagers, the spread of racism, alienated youth and the problems of male violence and alcoholism.

This generic infusion of subject material and locations typically associated with the 'observational' style of realist filmmaking is now widespread in contemporary British cinema. Whereas the traditional British social realist film tends to be loosely plotted, holding the viewer at a critical distance, many of the recent films are emotionally manipulative, have a narrative urgency and an aspiration to popular appeal. In films such as *Downtime* (1997) and *London to Brighton*, familiar stories about the economically marginalised and the victims of crime are inflected towards the thriller format through attributes of characterisation, visual style and structure. Similarly, the problematic cross-cultural romances of *Love + Hate* (2005) and *Ae Fond Kiss* share the narrative of escalating complication found in the romantic comedy, whilst *Mischief Night* (2006) features sequences that would not be out of place in a 'gross-out' teen comedy.

At the same time, the tradition of 'poetic' realism (most strongly associated with directors such as Bill Douglas and Terence Davies) has been continued by filmmakers who have drawn equal inspiration from British social realism and European art cinema. Gary Oldman's *Nil by Mouth* (1997) and the aforementioned impressionistic films of Lynne Ramsay and Pawel Pawlikowski, for example, all make distinctive use of editing, framing and sound design to suggest the inter-relationship of character and landscape. In the otherwise naturalistic *Wonderland*, *The Low Down* and *The Lawless Heart*, the psychological states of the protagonists are conveyed through time-lapse photography and freeze-frames, whereas *Orphans* (1997), *16 Years of Alcohol* (2003) and *The Lives of the Saints* (2006) have an expressionistic quality to their visual style and performances.

The history and costume film

From *The Private Life of Henry VIII* (1933) to *The Queen,* British cinema has been dominated by films that offer some kind of recreation of the past, whether based on historical events, literary sources or entirely imagined. Such is the commercial success of these films – and their ubiquity in both popular and academic surveys of the national cinema – it could be said that their historical emphasis is one of the defining characteristics of British film culture. However, as noted by scholars of film, literature and history, the representation of the past in recent British cinema is far from straightforward, and issues of genre, heritage and authenticity have been vigorously debated.

Although the majority of British films of the 1990s and 2000s have contemporary settings, 'period' or 'costume' films have played a disproportionately large role in the conceptualisation of British cinema as fundamentally backwards-looking. It is tempting to explain this apparent nostalgia (which is not the sole preserve of historical films) as a sign of the nation's cultural and political conservatism. Alternatively, this can be taken as verification of the role played by cultural history – shared stories, landscapes and artistic traditions – within definitions of Britain and Britishness.

There is critical agreement that the subject matter of the historically-set film 'involves a special relationship with notions of nationhood and national identity' (Chapman 2005: 6):

> The historical film raises questions such as whose history is being represented, by whom and for whom? The theme of identity is central to the genre: class, gender and specifically national identities are among its principal concerns. The historical film is not merely offering a representation of the past; in most instances it is offering a representation of a specifically national past. (Ibid.)

At the same time, the historical film can work – consciously or otherwise – to find contemporary resonance in its representation of a real or imagined past; it is taken for granted that the 'period' artefact is a valuable index of the present. As noted by James Chapman, films about real-life historical events such as *Chariots of Fire* and *Elizabeth* (1998) have only been an 'occasional presence' in British cinema since the 1970s, but they derive their cultural importance from coincidental contemporary events that had a 'major bearing on the ways they were understood, namely the Falklands War (*Chariots of Fire*) and the death of the Princess of Wales (*Elizabeth*)' (2005: 322).

More than simply revealing contemporary attitudes to the past, the historical film can also refashion and demythologise history. Deborah Cartmell and I. Q. Hunter use the term 'retrovision' to describe how some contemporary films have constructed 'countermyths', looking to the past sometimes with 'horror at its violence and oppression … and sometimes with nostalgia for lost innocence and style' (2001: 2). This trend for films that openly acknowledge their subjectivity of approach has become quite pronounced in recent years, with auteurs such as Mike Leigh, Ken Loach and Robert Altman contributing historical films in keeping with their own style and thematic preoccupations. The tendency for 'deconstructive' approaches to history reached a kind of zenith with *24 Hour Party People* (2002), a film about the Manchester music scene of the 1970s and 1980s that is 'unreadable' without an 'understanding of how times and places morph and shift' (Brabazon 2005: 139). It has also been taken as significant that British historical cinema (like historical fiction and television drama) has become fixated with periods of national 'greatness' such as the Elizabethan, Jacobean and Victorian eras, reflecting 'both a British desire to revisit history in the wake of new definitions of Britishness and a need to rethink the meaning of Englishness in a devolved nation now that England's myths have been degraded by revisionism' (Cartmell & Hunter 2001: 3).

The range of subject matter covered by British historical cinema suggests that it is best described as a tendency than as a coherent genre. However, in the contemporary context, British period films can be broadly divided into five (overlapping) categories: the literary adaptation (discussed in chapter 2), the 'biopic' of political, creative or everyday figures (which includes *Hilary and Jackie* (1998), *Pierrepoint* and *The Killing of John Lennon* (2006)), the monarchy film, the war film and representations of the twentieth century.

As noted by Kara McKechnie (2002) and others, the monarchy film makes up a small but significant area of British film production, undergoing 'periodic revival' (2002: 217), and re-modelling kings and queens 'according to the need of the age' (2002: 226). Thus, *Mrs Brown* (1997) and *Elizabeth* work to humanise their subjects through a representation that subverts their popular reputation as stern (and chaste) rulers; *Mrs Brown* addresses Queen Victoria's (Judi Dench) relationship with a Scottish servant John Brown (Billy Connolly) in the years following the death of her husband, whilst *Elizabeth* deviates from the conventional depiction of the Virgin Queen by showing her as a young, sexually active woman struggling to 'balance the public and personal' (Pigeon 2001: 15). Elizabeth I remains a source of fascination for contemporary filmmakers and audiences, being the subject of two recent British television serials – *Elizabeth I* (2005) and *The Virgin Queen* (2005) – and also appearing in *Shakespeare in Love*. Evidently, the age of imperial and creative supremacy with which she – like William Shakespeare – is associated provides a more appropriate setting for the monarchy film than times of doubt or constitutional crisis, the Civil War drama *To Kill a King* (2003) being a rare, and commercially unsuccessful, exception.

The machinery of myth-making: Cate Blanchett as the young queen in *Elizabeth*

Perhaps more than any other historical film in recent British cinema, the contemporary relevancies of *Elizabeth* received close – and sometimes contradictory – critical and journalistic readings, as discussed in detailed case studies of the film by Andrew Higson (2003) and James Chapman (2005). At a time of devolution, *Elizabeth* was read (and indeed promoted) as both a celebration and a critique of 'Englishness', an issue complicated by the film having an Indian director (Shekhar Kapur) and Australian star (Cate Blanchett). The death of the Princess of Wales during the making of the film prompted some commentators to draw contemporary parallels with troubled young royals in the public eye; Renée Pigeon, for example, suggests that the queen has the 'vulnerability of a Diana and the ruth-lessness of a Thatcher' (2001: 19). However, the film's exploration of the machinery of myth-making – exemplified by the sequence in which the young queen rehearses a well-known speech, as well as by the pictorial references to famous portraits – also resonated with the ideology of New Labour, suggesting how a 'reconceived history' might have 'practical effi-cacy in pre-millennium Britain' (Luckett 2000: 91):

> *Elizabeth* ... narrates a new history, one that reinforces the power of images over archival knowledge, and thereby legitimises a similar strategy for more contemporary narratives. The film might be seen in the context of Tony Blair's attempts to update the monarchy by

demonstrating how the *image* of a monarch might produce national renown even in the face of very real domestic problems and their potential threat to nationhood. (Ibid.)

This intervention between monarchy and a modernising New Labour government would be personified literally in *The Queen*, in which a newly-elected Blair urges Queen Elizabeth II to carry out a demonstrative act of public sympathy following the death of Princess Diana. Although the depiction of a living ruler gives the film an unusual *frisson*, in some respects *The Queen* is typical of the monarchy film in its exploration of the disjunction between public and private personae, as well as the platform it gives to a weighty performance more than an impersonation, this time by an actress with an international reputation (Helen Mirren).

Just as monarchy films speak to the present, so stories about wars have reflected shifting attitudes towards past and present conflict. Recent events have indicated that the UK still has an 'appetite for war' but wants to 'engage in a very different kind of war to what was on offer up until 1991' (Macallister 2004: 171). As discussed earlier, historical films about colonial conflict have tended to be read as critiques of contemporary foreign policy, but this new sensibility can be discerned more generally from the various films that offer a re-imagining of the 'paradigm conflict' of World War Two. According to Christopher Macallister, films such as *The English Patient*, *Charlotte Gray* and *Enigma* (2001) contribute to a 'new heroic grammar at odds with both earlier films and traditional understandings of war' (2004: 174). In line with current thinking about war, these films offer counter-myths that challenge gender roles, promote the personal above the political and are sceptical about heroic endeavour (heroic virtue being transplanted instead to safely 'fantastic' places such as the worlds of James Bond and Harry Potter). The role of women on the home front and in the field of conflict is acknowledged in *The Land Girls* (1998), *The War Bride* (2001), *Charlotte Gray*, *Enigma* and *Mrs Henderson Presents*. But the impulse to give voice to those traditionally excised from official histories has also resulted in films such as the animated *Valiant* (2005), *Two Men Went to War* (2002) and *The Rocket Post*, which consider the roles, respectively, of pigeon messengers, men deemed 'unfit' to serve and German scientists. Furthermore, there is emphasis upon the needs of the individual rather than the many; the heroine of *Charlotte Gray* ends up as a liaison operative for the French resistance through her quest to find her boyfriend, whereas one of the Bletchley Park code-breakers of *Enigma* is motivated by the need to discover the fate of his lover.

Although the period film is usually taken to refer to stories set in or before the early twentieth century, contemporary British cinema has often looked back to recent history, and with a degree of ambivalence. Whereas the historical film has been inclined to return to eras of supposed national coherence or achievement, there have been numerous family dramas set during times of social and cultural instability in the later twentieth century. To some extent, the depiction of racist attitudes between the 1960s and 1980s in *Wondrous Oblivion, East is East, Anita and Me* (2002) and *This is England* may reinforce perceptions of the 'backwardness' of the time, just as the 1950s-set *Vera Drake* and the 1980s-set *Billy Elliot* expose unenlightened attitudes towards class and gender roles. At the same time, a number of coming-of-age narratives work to explore their scenarios of social or ethnic division through stories about father-and-son reconciliations. This is the case in *Wondrous Oblivion*, in which David (Sam Smith), a Jewish boy living in suburban London, takes cricket lessons from Dennis (Delroy Lindo), a West Indian neighbour persecuted by local residents. In a fantasy of assimilation, his father Victor (Stanley Townsend), hitherto disinterested in his son's progress, eventually becomes part of a game that all three can play together (there is a similarly functioning scene at the end of *Bend It Like Beckham*). Sport also provides a foundational myth in *Sixty Six* (2006), in which Bernie (Gregg Sulkin), another Jewish boy, stands in danger of becoming excluded from a key moment of British social history when his Bar Mitzvah is scheduled at the same time as England's game in the World Cup final of 1966; not only are boy and father (Eddie Marsan) reconciled, but they manage – against the odds – to infiltrate Wembley Stadium, and thus the cultural mainstream.

Furthermore, some contemporary British films have sought to resurrect the spirit of past *cinematic* greatness, such as traditions of horror, Ealing comedy and the New Wave movement of the 1950s and early 1960s. With regard to the latter, *Vera Drake* reverses the standard gender balance of the kitchen-sink drama by giving voice and narrative space to a female character (see Hardy 2004), whilst *The Jealous God* (2005) is an adaptation of a John Braine novel from 1965 delivered in the style of the social realist cinema of the era.

Many of the films discussed above can be placed within a loosely-defined body of British heritage cinema. The term 'heritage film' was first used by Charles Barr in relation to 1940s films of 'British understatement and the rich British heritage' (1986: 12). But the term quickly become associated with a certain type of period drama that came to prominence in the 1980s. Typified by films such as *A Room with a View* (1985) and *Howards End* (1992), the heritage text was commonly understood as a film that drew upon a work of classic literature, dwelt upon the lives and properties of the upper classes and was set roughly in the period between 1860 and World War Two. The so-called 'heritage debate' that ensued amongst scholars of British film culture initially called attention to their political implications, with some commentators deeming them to be nostalgic and conservative within the context of reactionary Thatcherite ideology. But further analysis, prompted by feminist and gay readings, led to more nuanced and varied positions on their gender politics, their appeal to audiences, their umbilical link with the 'heritage' industries and their generic delineation and coherence.[3]

Critical work on the heritage film has also queried the extent to which the term can still be applied to more recently made British period films. Pamela Church Gibson (2000), Claire Monk (2002) and others have suggested how some films of the 1990s such as *The Wings of the Dove*, *Elizabeth* and *Shakespeare in Love* depart from the 'canonical' heritage film through their visual style, hybridised form, self-conscious foregrounding of questions of myth-making and historical representation, and their appeal to contemporary sensibilities. Many of these qualities are also hallmarks of period films from the early twenty-first century such as the biopics *Pandaemonium* and *Becoming Jane*.

In relation to *Elizabeth* and the gleefully anachronistic *Shakespeare in Love*, Julianne Pidduck proposes that they mark a 'postmodern turn in the British period drama', allowing a 'playful, performative sensibility' to overtake the 'realist mode' (2007: 172). Furthermore, 'against a British heritage tradition premised on precise dialogue, pastoral *mise-en-scène* and subtle dramas of love and class distinction, these Elizabethan films employ the lexicon of corporeality and sensuality' (ibid.).

It has been argued that films such as *The Wings of the Dove*, *The Tichborne Claimant* (1998) and *Mansfield Park* (1999) are more 'progressive' in their registering of contemporary debates around sexual and cultural politics (see Wood 1999; Gibson 2004; Dave 2006: 36–40). However, the deployment of the term 'post-heritage' to categorise these and other films has not been universally welcomed, as this carries the implication that previous examples of the heritage film were incapable of radicalism in intention or interpretation. Furthermore, British film culture has long known a strain of iconoclastic or deliberately 'inauthentic' approaches to history, from the avant-garde contributions of Derek Jarman and Peter Greenaway to the 'vulgar' work of Ken Russell and the Carry On films.[4] However, even though the term 'heritage film' has always had far greater currency in academia than among audiences or within the industry, the 'marketing, promotion and indeed textual strategies of recent British period films ... have worked hard, and with considerable strategic sophisti-cation, to project the films as "not heritage films"' (Monk 2002: 193). Some examples, such as *The Revengers Tragedy* and *A Cock and Bull Story*, could even be identified as 'anti-heritage' in their self-conscious subversion and parody of the expectations of a period film.

A further point of contention is the efficacy of applying the 'heritage' paradigm – conceived at first to interrogate the relation of the period dramas of the 1980s to Thatcherite ideology – to the films of the Labour era. Noting how the differing conditions from the mid-1990s onwards have implications for the 'ideological substance' of the heritage film, as well as the 'currency' of the critical debate around it, Monk proposes that the heritage aesthetic (and its ideological function) has more recently been embraced by underclass films and romantic comedies (2002: 195). Certainly, in their selective social vision and enthralment to the pastoral, films such as *Notting Hill* and *Bridget Jones's Diary* could well be labelled 'contemporary' heritage films. Such questions about the representation of modern Britain will be the focus of the following chapter.

4   REPRESENTING CONTEMPORARY BRITAIN

This chapter considers the ways in which British cinema has represented the perspectives and experiences of those dwelling in (or merely passing through) contemporary Britain, and thereby provides a means – one of many, it should be stressed – of gauging the currency of the national film culture. The film scholar and the cultural historian share an interest in how British cinema has responded to (and in some cases intervened in) wider debates around sexuality, class, gender and ethnicity, with contemporary representations merely the latest manifestation of a long-running dialogue between a cinema, its people and the world at large.

Understandably, scrutiny and significance have tended to be given most to the projection of voices that are held to be in some way non-dominant, whether in terms of British cinematic traditions, or in British society more generally (or both). This is not to suggest that all films giving some kind of platform to 'minority' viewpoints are duty bound to be pioneering or to have a deliberately corrective agenda. Nonetheless, the presence (or absence) of people from non-dominant groups behind and in front of the camera is crucial to any assessment of the scope of a national cinema.

This chapter offers individual sections on the representation of sexuality, class, gender and ethnicity in contemporary British cinema. The danger of a single-issue approach is that it contradicts what cultural theorists have told us about the complex, multifaceted nature of identity. Besides, few films are made with the sole purpose of exploring one particular aspect of cultural identity, and some of the most interesting films of modern British cinema, from *My Beautiful Laundrette* (1985) to *A Way of Life*, have been those situated on the interstices of identity politics. Furthermore, there are other areas of representation that also merit scrutiny, even if space forbids here, such as the depiction of people with disabilities, or with different professions, ages, religious beliefs and political persuasions.

Sexuality

British cinema's chaste reputation as a place where 'the stiff upper lip has tended to triumph over the stiff anything else' (M. Williams 2006: 59) has only been partly challenged by the films of the 1990s and 2000s. In response to *Kinky Boots*, merely one of a brace of comic films about stripping and/or gender-troubling activity that includes *The Full Monty* and *Calendar Girls* (2003), Daniel Jays saw 'another British film that approaches an erotically charged subject only to render it almost entirely sexless' (2005: 74). Although sexual desire is a persistent theme across recent British cinema, it is usually dealt with in a manner that is either overly flippant – as in the case of comedies like *Sex Lives of the Potato Men* and *Preaching to the Perverted* (1997) – or joylessly earnest. In films that push the boundaries of sexual frankness such as *Under the Skin* (1997), *Intimacy, The Principles of Lust* (2003) and *Red Road*, sexual desire is portrayed as fundamentally self-destructive or used as an index of transgression or pathology.

Contemporary British cinema's bold, if somewhat pleasure-free attitude towards sexuality has exhibited itself in assorted ways. The erotic desires of the elderly have been explored in *The Mother* (2003) and *Venus* – both scripted by Hanif Kureishi – but also registered by *Calendar Girls* and *Ladies in Lavender*, whilst *Song of Songs* (2006) was concerned with an incestuous relationship between a brother and sister. There have also been a great many films, some with more serious intentions than others, about the workings of the sex industry and its appeal to its workers and customers. Among these are *The Escort, Last Resort, Rabbit Fever, The Gigolos* (2006) and *Everything* (2004), in which a man frequents a prostitute to understand why his daughter chose this profession.

Groundbreakingly explicit: Margo Stilley and Kieran O'Brien in *9 Songs*

Although not the first British mainstream film to contain unsimulated sexual imagery, Michael Winterbottom's groundbreakingly explicit *9 Songs*, released in 2004, was a delayed and controversial response to the trend for graphic sexual content in independent cinema worldwide. Telling the story of a relationship exclusively through a couple's sexual encounters and gig-going experiences, *9 Songs* was a pioneering attempt to 'claim the realistic depiction of explicit sexual activity for "normal films"' (M. Williams 2006: 59). Although given a respectful reception, in the main, the film was also deemed somewhat 'stereotypical' (2005: 42) and 'surprisingly retrograde' (M. Williams 2006: 62) in its representation of its enigmatic female character Lisa (Margot Stilley) primarily through her sexual desires.

The prominence of homosexual characters within contemporary British cinema, and the significance of their representation, is open to question. There has been little in the way of niche cinema aimed predominantly at non-heterosexual audiences, but nor have there been many 'cross-over' films foregrounding gay or bisexual characters. A significant difference between the gay-themed cinema of the Blair era and that of previous decades is its dispersal across a range of genres, including romantic comedies, heritage films, gangster capers, biopics and youth films. Although these films tend to refrain from direct political commentary, their drive to assimilate homosexuality within the cinematic mainstream is paralleled by its political 'normalisation' during the time of Blair's office through acts such as the equalisation of the age of consent, the outlawing of workplace discrimination on grounds of sexuality and the legal recognition of same-sex civil partnerships. However, the critical and commercial under-performance of most of the 'queer' films of the period has meant that homosexual representation remains a peripheral aspect of British film culture.

In contrast to the diversity of gay-themed films in the 2000s, the majority of those produced in the mid-1990s tended to fall into one of two categories. The relationship between a homosexual artist and his lover/muse is considered in *Love and Death on Long Island* (1997), *Wilde* (1997), *Love is the Devil* and the quasi-biographical glam fantasy *Velvet Goldmine*, whereas *Beautiful Thing* (1996) and *Get Real* (1998) are feelgood fairy tales about anguished adolescents looking for love and social acceptance. Deemed by some to be typical of the 'anodyne positivism' (Griffiths 2006: 15) of the British queer cinema of the 1990s weighed down by the post-AIDS burden of political correctness, *Beautiful Thing* and *Get Real* do seem designed primarily to offer hope and positive role-models to young gay and lesbian audiences. More nuanced readings, however, have been attentive to the way in which they describe a complex topography of 'queer and non-queer spaces' (see Fouz-Hernández 2003) and expose the mixed messages within contemporary gay politics about assimilation versus separation (see Nowlan 2006).

Later films with a comparable 'coming out' scenario, such as *Chicken Tikka Masala* (2004), *Imagine Me and You* and *Gypo*, featured significantly older characters, and displaced the problem of social acceptance onto issues of cultural conflict and individual desire. Similarly, the adolescent lesbian romance of *My Summer of Love* is depicted as a holiday crush rather than as an epiphanous moment in the characters' development.

Whilst these films de-emphasise their homosexual theme, some reviewers were struck by the 'gayness' of *The History Boys* (see Rayns 2006), especially in comparison with its original theatrical version by Alan Bennett. Rather than focusing on the distress of sexual confusion, the film sets out to illustrate, in the words of Hector (Richard Griffiths), a teacher who gropes his sixth form students when they ride on his motorbike, how the 'transmission of knowledge is in itself an erotic act'. In contrast to the climate of 'queer-baiting' depicted in the aforementioned teenage 'coming out' films, *The History Boys* portrays its young characters as indulgent of their teacher's foibles, and accepting of Posner (Samuel Barnett), the only openly gay member of the class and his yearning for the school pin-up Dakin (Dominic Cooper). As with the lesbian romance *Nina's Heavenly Delights*, the film treats homosexuality in a matter-of-fact way that could be construed as progressive.

Examples of the political and cultural sanction given to non-heterosexuality by the newly-elected New Labour government in 1997 include the invitation of 'queer' celebrities to 10 Downing Street and the promotion of openly gay cabinet members and MPs. Hopes were raised for the renaissance of a subversive, experimental queer cinema not simply concerned with validating 'alternative' sexualities and increasing tolerance but demonstrating a capacity to 'shock and unsettle the indifferent (hereto-) mainstream cinematic establishment' (Griffiths 2006: 16). Falling into this category were Duncan Roy's autobiographical *AKA* and Lisa Gornick's low-budget lesbian romance *Do I Love You?* (2003), two personal projects that acknowledge the fluid nature of identity. In Roy's film, working-class teenager Dean Page (Matthew Leitch) impersonates a lord and becomes a figure of fascination for an effete set of aristocrats and hangers-on, but his capacity for sexual union with same-sex partners is hampered by traumatic recollections of his abusive father, and his exposure results in a prison sentence. *Do I Love You?* presents a thirtysomething woman (played by the director) addressing her crisis of identity and lack of productivity (as both a woman and a writer) through meetings with past lovers and conversations with her sophisticated circle of London acquaintances. The question posed by her sexually inquisitive father – 'what do lesbians do?' – is answered in part by the professions of her friends, which include an artist, a journalist, a therapist and an opera singer; the film makes it perfectly clear that, to quote her father again, 'there's quite a bit of it around'.

Lab Ky Mo's outrageously camp *9 Dead Gay Guys* offers a more simplistic deconstruction of cultural stereotypes, taking gleeful, taboo-breaking pleasure in the cartoonish presentation of one-dimensional characters such as the miserly rabbi Golders Green, the well-endowed West African Brothers and the sexually inadequate Desperate Dwarf.

As a parody of Guy Ritchie's gangster capers, *9 Dead Gay Guys* is part of a broader trend for the 'queering' of popular British genres. The literary/ heritage drama and biopic have provided space for homosexual representation since the 1980s, and hence *Wilde*, *Bright Young Things* (2003) and *Stage Beauty* are continuing a path trodden already by *Maurice* (1987) and *Prick Up Your Ears* (1987). But a newer development is the queer re-imagining of the romantic comedy genre, as illustrated by the boy-meets-boy and girl-meets-girl stories of *Different for Girls* (1996), *Bedrooms and Hallways* (1998), *Imagine Me and You* and *Nina's Heavenly Delights*. However, despite being pitched at mainstream audiences, these films did not have the impact of those such as *The Full Monty* and *Billy Elliot*, where homosexual characters are mostly pushed to the fringes – either to offer a variation on the theme of troubled masculinity (*The Full Monty*), or to dislodge any anxieties that the main protagonist might be gay (*Billy Elliot*). The removal of a lesbian relationship from initial screenplay drafts of *Bend It Like Beckham* adds further evidence of a squeamishness about homosexual representation in mainstream comedies and dramas. Two further examples can be cited. In *Kinky Boots*, a staid footwear business is energised through the input of a transvestite despite the homophobia of the workplace, but the film itself ignores the possibility of a same-sex relationship for its main character. The marginalisation of the gay experience to one single plot strand of several in *Scenes of a Sexual Nature* (2006), a film set entirely on Hampstead Heath, is also surprising, given the location's fame as a night-time spot for cruising.

Class

It is a truism that British cinema is riven with the class consciousness that defines the national character more generally. According to the results of a poll carried out by the *Guardian* newspaper in October 2007, ten years of Labour rule had apparently failed to create a classless society, with social mobility occurring at a slower rate than hoped for by politicians, and a 'huge majority certain that their social standing determines the way they are judged' (Glover 2007). However, the poll also brought attention to the paradox that whilst Britain was still divided by social status, 'the cultural influence of the middle class has never been greater' (Aitkenhead 2007). This uncertainty over social status is deeply ingrained within British film culture, which remains unsure whether the nation's class hierarchy is its greatest asset or its utmost shame, something of export value (in the case of heritage films or 'underclass' comedies) or something to be challenged or transcended. Furthermore, British cinema of the Blair years has only partly been 'on message' with New Labour's 'virtual ban on thinking or speaking of class relations, or class agency, or class as a still meaningful category of analysis' (Kaplan 2004: 101).

Even the most cursory survey of contemporary output reveals a plethora of films in which the disparities or complexities of the class system play either a central or subtextual role. The plight of the underclass has been a preoccupation for filmmakers working within the social realist mode, but there have also been numerous thrillers, comedies and historical films predicated upon the intransigency of social boundaries. Stories of class mobility or aspiration are told in films as varied as *The Tichborne Claimant*, *Ali G Indahouse*, *AKA* and *Match Point*, whilst the plots of *My Brother Tom* (2001), *Gosford Park*, *Lassie*, *Greyfriars Bobby* (2005), *Atonement* and countless others are constructed upon problematic relationships between characters positioned differently on the social scale.

Diagnoses of class friction have been embedded within a number of films intended (wholly or partly) as 'state-of-the-nation' critiques. In Anthony Minghella's *Breaking and Entering* (2006), Miro (Rafi Gavron), the son of a Bosnian refugee, breaks into the newly-built Kings Cross offices of an architectural practice involved in a regeneration scheme for this formerly disreputable but now socially complex area. The robbery brings the architects Will (Jude Law) and Sandy (Martin Freeman) – who conform to the stereotype of the neurotic, dissatisfied middle-class professional – into initially uncomfortable but ultimately enlightening contact with the types of local resident presumed to be the beneficiaries of their urban planning strategies: asylum seekers, economic migrants, manual workers, prostitutes and so forth. Will confesses that he prefers 'talking in metaphors', but his journey from chilly professional and family spaces (he has a depressive Scandinavian wife and an autistic child) to the more humane world of Anne (Juliette Binoche), the cultured (she is a classical pianist) but financially desperate Bosnian mother, is itself a metaphor for the bourgeois theorist forced into a confrontation with 'reality'. Will's colleague Sandy is thrown into similar anguish when suspicion for the robbery falls upon Erika (Caroline Chikezie), the black office cleaner for whom he harbours romantic feelings. In other words, *Breaking and Entering* is more insightful as a film about the unease of the professional middle-classes than as a nuanced social mapping of multicultural London.

In this way, Minghella's film invites comparison with *Notting Hill*, which also positions its middle-class characters within an area of the capital commonly associated with ethnic and social diversity. In *Breaking and Entering*, Will's architectural plans for Kings Cross may be abstract, but they are at least progressive in their inclusivity. In contrast, the Hugh Grant character in *Notting Hill* seems part of an *embourgoisement* project (shared by the filmmakers) to reclaim this corner of London as a pastoral, fairy tale territory where cultured under-achievers can prosper without fear of economic hardship.

Away from London, an altogether different strategy of transformation is set in motion by Tony Wilson (as impersonated by Steve Coogan) in *24 Hour Party People*. In showing Wilson's involvement with the Factory record label, and then the Hacienda club, the film supports the hypothesis that the Cambridge-educated Wilson had been an important figure in the cultural regeneration of Manchester, a staunchly industrial northern city. Comic value is derived from the illogicality of a flamboyant, self-consciously intellectual figure playing a role in the promotion of pop music, a form most associated with working-class authenticity: in this case, punk, new wave and the 'Madchester' rave scene.

24 Hour Party People is only one of a number of films to draw satirical energy from class 'tourism'. The perpetually-thwarted social climber has long been a stock character in British television comedy and sitcoms, but in recent years these aspirational figures have been complemented by characters bent instead upon downward mobility. Giving platforms to comic creations familiar to British television audiences, *Kevin & Perry Go Large* and *Ali G Indahouse* ridicule the appropriation of 'lad' and 'urban' culture by suburbanites and their offspring. But one of the most resonant and politically astute images of social slumming can be found in *The Queen*, where Prime Minister Tony Blair is seen at home wearing a Newcastle United football shirt. The requisition of certain aspects of traditional working-class culture, such as football, by the professional classes in the 1990s found expression in various ways, but most notably through the promotion of 'lad' culture (epitomised by the success of *Loaded* magazine).

In the 1990s, the representation of working-class experience reached prominence through a number of films that shared an interest in issues of exclusion and unemployment. These films provided some of the decade's most iconic images of British cinema: Robert Carlyle and friends practising their 'Chippendales' stripping act in the dole queue in *The Full Monty* (a scene famously replicated publicly by Prince Charles); Ewan McGregor emerging triumphant out of a filthy lavatory bowl with his pill in *Trainspotting*; Pete

Postlethwaite rising from his hospital bed to lead his pit band to victory at the Royal Albert Hall in *Brassed Off*. In many respects, these moments of simultaneous desperation and transformation are indicative of the mixed messages given by the films and their popular reception. By entrenching stories and imagery of marginalisation and poverty in the popular imagination, the films contradict any political proclamation of a classless, undivided society at the turn of the millennium. At the same time, and despite their occasionally bleak content, there is a 'utopian' quality to some of these films (see Hill 2000), particularly those that describe the playful, energetic strategies adopted by marginalised men to ward off disenfranchisement.

These films, and their complex relation to the 'socio-political landscape of post-industrial Britain' (Ashby & Higson 2000: 247) have received close critical scrutiny. For example, in her categorisation of a loose-knit, genre-straddling cycle of 'underclass films' – ranging from *Trainspotting* and *The Full Monty* to *Lock, Stock and Two Smoking Barrels*, *Twenty Four Seven* and *Nil by Mouth* – Claire Monk (2000b) draws upon a controversial term most associated with neo-conservative political theorists such as Charles Murray. However, Monk distances herself from their definition of the 'underclass' as parasitical and work-shy, utilising instead a more neutral description of a '*post-working* class that owes its existence to the economic and social damage wrought by globalisation, local industrial decline, the restructuring of the labour market and other legacies of the Thatcher era' (2000b: 274; emphasis in original).

Cora Kaplan argues that *Brassed Off*, *The Full Monty* and *Billy Elliot* – northern-set films that chronicle the effects of the dismantling of heavy industry and the destruction of union power by the Conservative governments of the 1980s and 1990s – all resonate with the 'revisionist politics of New Labour and its political allies' (2004: 95):

> Each film in different ways describes the decline and 'death' of an old social, economic and political order as lived in the provincial cities and towns of England – almost exclusively white, Anglo England – a world each of them selectively evokes, but with fluctuating registers of regret or nostalgia. (Ibid.)

Giving endorsement to 'performance' (see Wayne 2006b) – in the literal sense of a public show upon a stage – as a means of empowerment, these

The effects of unemployment: Gaz (Robert Carlyle) and friends in *The Full Monty*

films would seem to reflect a desire for restored communities, but the extent of their political commitment has been called into question.

In *The Full Monty*, a group of former steelyard workers are characterised by the different ways that unemployment has affected their spatial and bodily power. The central figure, Gaz (Robert Carlyle), is unable to provide financial support for his son (William Snape), and is barred from the prosperous home of his estranged wife (Emily Woof); the other characters face equivalent humiliations, from impotence to anxieties over sexuality. Locked out of places of work, family and even leisure – the final straw being the appropriation of the working men's club for a female-only stripping event – and left to roam the streets like children, the men embark on a strategy of reclamation: the perfection of a stripping routine to be performed in the same club. As has been pointed out by Monk (2000a) and others, however, this is as much a masculinist project to reclaim former spaces of male dominance, as it is an expression of class solidarity. Furthermore, in its freezing of the image at the moment of triumph – the men removing their underwear in front of an enthusiastic female audience – the film can only offer a temporary solution to the deep-rooted problems diagnosed in the narrative.

But the story of *The Full Monty* was in effect continued and completed through the film's appropriation by politicians, commentators and cultural theorists. Noting the impact of the film on British popular culture, Kelly

Farrell suggests how *The Full Monty* 'feeds not only into a sense of crisis of masculinity but into the perception of a *fin de millennium* crisis of British national, post-imperial identity' (2003: 119–20):

> Pressed into national service, the comic nature of *The Full Monty* wholly eradicates any political pressure for concrete social change. Questions about the actual state of masculine identity, not to mention the issue of long-term unemployment, are cemented over with the bricks and mortar of a satisfying narrative closure, both intradiegetically and in the text of Blair's political posturing. (2003: 133)

Farrell notes how the film was used to serve the political purposes of Tony Blair and the Prince of Wales, but also how its very particular story of northern unemployment was 'appropriated as a seemingly unlikely fantasy of British imperial (re)empowerment' (2003: 120).

Another small-scale but symbolic strategy of reclamation is attempted by the two young Newcastle United fans of *Purely Belter*. Unemployed and unable to afford season tickets, Gerry (Chris Beattie) and Sewell (Greg McLane) can only fantasise about re-entry to St James' Park football ground, the communal space that has traditionally been a symbol of (male) working-class culture. Their fund-raising tactics take the form of increasingly bold and desperate raids on the sites of leisure, commerce and affluence they are otherwise excluded from: they become shoplifters and eventually bank robbers. So, *Purely Belter* records the 'shiny new privatised landscape of English football' (Kelly 2000: 61), and communicates how processes of privatisation have alienated a working-class fan base.[1] The film fosters awareness of those left behind by the gentrification and diversification of the game, a process reflected and indeed promoted by films such as the adaptation of Nick Hornby's *Fever Pitch* and the internationally successful *Bend It Like Beckham*.

One of the most noteworthy films about class 'betterment' is *Billy Elliot*, yet another film to suggest how performance – here, ballet dancing – can be a means of empowerment. However, in contrast with the collective activities of *The Full Monty* and *Brassed Off*, the ten-year-old Billy (Jamie Bell) works towards a very personal triumph. Set in a northern mining town during the strike of 1984, but with hardly any explicit discussion of the causes of industrial action, the film uses the brutal clashes

An emblem of economic rejuvenation?: Jamie Bell as the boy who learns ballet in *Billy Elliot*

between police and strikers merely as a trigger (and possible justification) for Billy's escapist urges. The instinctively aggressive responses of Billy's father Jackie (Gary Lewis) and brother Tony (Jamie Draven) to his newfound interest in a suspiciously non-masculine endeavour also carry accusations of class treachery, on a par with the 'scab' workers who break the strikes.

Responding to its narrative of regeneration, John Hill describes how 'in a loose allegory of the transition from a manufacturing to a service-based economy, Billy becomes an emblem of economic rejuvenation through participation in the "creative industries"' (2004: 108). Far from being the one out of step, Billy is a pioneer, introducing a model for adaptation for the post-industrial age; the film's various dance sequences show him literally transforming his environment through exploratory movements. However, any regional development is left unaddressed by the ending, which positions the adult Billy, now a star of the ballet world, on a theatrical stage – an indeterminate space, with connotations of both egalitarianism and elite culture. The young Billy is last seen trying unsuccessfully to communicate with his brother from the back of the bus that takes him to ballet school. The insurmountable distance between the provinces and the cosmopolitan centre is emphasised by the disorientation of Billy's family when they come to London to see him perform.

Billy Elliot thus provides another example of an evasive conclusion falling somewhere between realism and myth. But echoing the critical work that has read some British romantic comedies as reassuring 'fairy tales' (see chapter 3), Judith Lancioni notes how *Billy Elliot* uses a 'Cinderella motif' – that is, the story of a 'motherless child at odds with her unappreci- ated family but still able to preserve her sense of compassion and a strong work ethic' (2006: 709–10) – as a 'vehicle for expressing a hope that might otherwise be dismissed as beyond the realm of possibility' (2006: 727). However, for Paul Marris, *Billy Elliot* and *The Full Monty* were emblematic of the 'retrenchment' of British cinema's representational tradition of 'north- ern realism' to a state of 'decadent mannerism' (2001: 49). In referring back to the de-industrialising project of the Thatcher years, these 'delayed 1980s films' (Hill 1999: 168) can 'afford their retrospective feel-good humour and warmth, because the battles have been fought and the hard choices made' (ibid.). But this backward glance 'no longer permits the North and the "state of the nation" to be addressed with freshness, vigour and insight' (Marris 2001: 49).

By and large, British cinema's interest in the collective activities of the disenfranchised has waned in recent years, to be replaced by a new inter- est in cross-cultural relationships and the problem of racism. While films such as *A Way of Life*, *Love + Hate* (2005), *Wondrous Oblivion* and *This is England* have been commended for confronting issues of contemporane- ous relevance, their cumulative effect may also be to define racism as a phenomenon unique to working-class communities. However sympathetic these films are to the cultural and economic pressures faced by their protagonists, the espousal of illiberal attitudes by some characters may reinforce wider prejudices about a feckless, ignorant underclass.

In a similar way, the bawdy, carnivalesque tone of Penny Woolcock's Leeds-set *Mischief Night*, with its feral children, black humour and flip- pant treatment of contentious subjects such as paedophilia and 'jihad videos', can be viewed as a life-affirming celebration of 'chav' culture in the style of the popular television series *Shameless*, and also as a far more inclusive representation of regional community than those offered in previous decades.[2] British films about the working class, or more recently, the underclass, have tended to stray no further than the expe- riences of white, heterosexual males; the central character of *Mischief Night*, like that of *A Way of life*, is a young mother (played by Kelli Hollis), and the film also places a spotlight on children and members of the Asian community. Yet *Mischief Night* can also be perceived as ammunition for the politicians and commentators who have demonised certain areas of multicultural Britain as the lawless terrain of 'hoodies', single mothers and would-be terrorists.

Men

On the whole, British cinema is still dominated by narratives of male experience and endeavour, and the range of representation defies easy summary. The emasculated 'dinosaur' of the underclass films shares a crowded stage with the pathological revenger (*Dead Man's Shoes*), the 'wounded' male cut adrift from family (*Orphans*), the 'manchild' frozen in adolescence (*About a Boy*) and the newly resurrected action hero overcoming horrific physical torment (*Casino Royale*).

However, across the numerous films with male-centred subject matter, the contested place of men within families and communities is a persistent anxiety. In the 1990s, and to a much lesser extent the 2000s, stories about men under pressure banding together to regain dignity became a staple of British cinema. Many of these, such as *Brassed Off* and *One For the Road* brought a patina of social commentary to their narratives of male collectivity, but others, like the football dramas *The Match* and *Mean Machine*, and some of the more lightweight gangster capers, were straightforward genre films with no apparent subtextual agenda.

As noted, a repeated scenario is the adoption of a non-masculine 'performance' as part of a strategy of improvement. The gender-bending conceits of *The Full Monty* and *Billy Elliot* found an echo in a trio of prison-set comedies in which a female authority figure coaxes a reluctant group of men to exercise their creativity. However, if many of the underclass films described characters trying to re-animate male spaces and bonds, *Greenfingers* (2000), *Lucky Break* and the television film *Tomorrow La Scala!* (2002) suggest how the 'feminised' hobbies of amateur musical theatre and gardening can provide both a literal and figurative strategy of escape from confinement.

The feelgood endings of these films, with their emphasis on restored homosocial bonds and victorious performance, were answered by a number of films that sought to interrogate rather than celebrate the activities of the male 'gang' and to reveal the innate aggression of communal missions. However, if the representations of violent masculinity in the likes of *Nil by Mouth* and *This is England* seemed to invite critique, the casting of charismatic performers and the emphasis on the charms (as well as the evils) of gang life gave the films a degree of ambivalence towards their subjects and their lifestyle. In *The Football Factory* and *Green Street* (2004), for example, listless young men are drawn to the camaraderie and violence of the football hooligan subculture in equal measure. In the absence of editorial condemnation, both films risk accusations of glamorising thuggery and promoting one of the UK's less respectable exports. The concluding section of *Green Street*, in which exiled journalism student Matt Buckner (Elijah Wood) returns to the US to seek vengeance on his roommate and push forward his writing career, suggests that his brief stint amongst the West Ham 'firm' has been his true education in manliness: as he says at the start, 'What I was about to learn, no Ivy League school could teach me.' There is a similar ambiguity of message in *The Football Factory*, Nick Love's adaptation of John King's 1996 novel about Chelsea fans. With its arsenal of subjective devices – dream sequences, captions, voice-overs and so on – the film is stylistically lively and suggestive of the adrenaline rush of the hooligan lifestyle; tellingly, the film was co-produced with Rockstar Games, best known for their controversially violent *Grand Theft Auto* and *Manhunt* series.

The familiar narrative of men bound together under pressure was given a reactionary recapitulation in *Outlaw*, also directed by Nick Love. Incensed by an apparent breakdown in law and order, and the impotence of the police, a cuckolded ex-paratrooper (played by Sean Bean) brings together a gang of crime victims to deliver rough justice to the gangsters and thugs who wronged them. With its keynote speeches about the prevalence of 'paedophiles, dealers, bullies, junkies, scum', and its accompanying website featuring games where players could take pot-shots at 'nonces' such as Ian Huntley and Gary Glitter, *Outlaw* wears its tabloid heart on its sleeve, and provoked swift condemnation. Writing in the *Times* newspaper, James Mottram described it as the 'most incendiary British film since Stanley Kubrick's *A Clockwork Orange*' (2007), and Wendy Ide expressed anxiety that Love may be inflaming something 'simmering in the nation's psyche' (2007).

The animosity directed at *Outlaw* from the broadsheet press and elsewhere can partly be explained through the recognition that Love's films – which include *Goodbye Charlie Bright* (2001), *The Football Factory* and *The*

The charms and evils of male camaraderie: Sean (Thomas Turgoose) and gang in
This is England

Business – have proven more capable of speaking to parts of the British
public about the contemporary pressures upon working-class men than
the films of other more 'respectable', socially committed directors such
as Ken Loach and Shane Meadows. Indeed, Love is one of the most commercially successful of UK directors: *The Football Factory* had a budget of
£500,000 but sold nearly a million copies on DVD.

A more personal take on the masculine propensity for aggression
and alcoholic dependency is evident in films by Richard Jobson, Gary
Oldman and Shane Meadows based upon their own lives and family
backgrounds. Whilst Jobson's *16 Years of Alcohol* derives from the experiences of himself and his brother, and Oldman's semi-autobiographical
Nil by Mouth is offered as a tribute to his father, *This is England* represents Shane Meadows' autobiographical take on his own dalliance with
'skinhead' culture as a boy in the early 1980s. The film's main character,
Shaun (Thomas Turgoose), had a father who was killed in the Falklands
conflict and, as with the other films, *This is England* describes how male
camaraderie provides succour and subcultural identity – for example,
through fashion and musical taste – for 'fatherless' men, but also how it
can indoctrinate hatred for the outsider. Through the character of Combo
(Stephen Graham), a charismatic racist who wrestles control of the group
and promotes a far-right political stance, the film implies that extreme

nationalism stems from the same psychological wellspring as the craving to be part of a gang. Combo's horrific attack on the black character Milky (Andrew Shim) appears to be an envious response to the latter's idyllic description of being part of a coherent, nurturing community.

The problematic relationship between men (or boys) and father figures is a key motif of Meadows' films, cropping up also in *Twenty Four Seven*, *A Room for Romeo Brass* and *Dead Man's Shoes*. But it is also a theme that continues to dominate British cinema more generally, from *Liam* (2000) to *And When Did You Last See Your Father?* (2007). Tensions between parents and children are often portrayed for purely melodramatic purpose, but as indicated in *This is England*, where the matter of racism is subsumed within a power struggle between 'good' and 'bad' fathers, parental relations are often used to explore – and sometimes to evade – schisms of class and cultural identity. There are several examples of films in which men are characterised and judged by their relationship with children, or through their role as mentor figures. As Cora Kaplan notes, the ultimate reconciliation of fathers and sons from 'dying working-class communities' in *The Full Monty*, *Brassed Off* and *Billy Elliot* provides feelgood conclusions but also works to 'deny the fissures within these communities and the unbridgeable rifts, becoming wider, between the "two nations"' (2004: 110). What is more, these reconciliations are illusory: the failing fathers of these films – unemployed or in ailing health – can only temporarily win the respect of their offspring, if at all.

Indeed, the father figure's realisation of his impotence frequently surfaces, as it does in *My Name is Joe*, *My Son the Fanatic*, *On a Clear Day* and *The Darkest Light*. Across these films, fathers are haunted by their inability to rescue a young man from the clutches of gangsters and religious extremists, or their failure to save a child from drowning or perishing from cancer. Meanwhile, in *Afterlife* (2003), *Dear Frankie* (2004), *About a Boy*, *The Lives of the Saints* and *The One and Only*, men connoted as professionally-orientated, narcissistic or otherwise unreconstructed are humanised through becoming a mentor to young boys (or in the case of *Afterlife* and *The One and Only*, a young African girl, and a woman with Down's Syndrome).

The necessity for transformed masculinity is stressed through the characterisation of unmoveable patriarchs in *East is East*, *Love + Hate* and *Alpha Male* (2006), the loathsome paedophiles seen or referred to in *A Kind of*

Hush (1999), *The Lost Son*, *Kidulthood* and *London to Brighton*, and the demonic fathers of *The War Zone*, *Hold Back the Night* (1999) and *AKA* who obscenely violate the sanctity of the family unit through the sexual abuse of their teenage children. A more ambivalent representation of authoritative responsibility is given by *Gregory's Two Girls* (1999) and *The History Boys*, where taboo-breaking teacher-pupil relationships are used to raise wider questions about educational and political intervention.

The narratives of parental guilt or failure told largely from the adult perspective are answered by child-centred scenarios of rescue. In family films such as *Stormbreaker* (2006), *Thunderpants* (2002), *There's Only One Jimmy Grimble* (2000) and the *Harry Potter* series, young boy heroes act out the fantasies of their target audiences in saving the world, the space race, or – more modestly – the school football team; elsewhere there are 'angelic' children working to restore families and communities. In the realist dramas *Pure* (2002) and *Sweet Sixteen*, a young boy and teenager are bent on saving their mothers from heroin addiction, whilst the more fanciful *Gabriel and Me* (2001) and *Millions* (2004) portray children in direct communion with saintly advisors.

Women

Within contemporary British cinema, male-centred films far outnumber those told from a female perspective, making the identification of particular cycles more difficult. That said, questions of feminine agency have frequently been raised across films of differing genres and historical settings. Literary and period dramas such as *Elizabeth* and *Charlotte Gray* have celebrated the role played by women in history, and the contributions of female artists and writers have also been celebrated in biopics like *Hilary and Jackie*, *Iris* and *Miss Potter*. Issues pertaining to the female body, such as infertility and abortion, have been contemplated, to differing ends, in *Mad Cows* (1999), *Fanny and Elvis* (1999), *Felicia's Journey* and *Vera Drake*. Furthermore, the rising number of female directors and writers contributing to British film culture, and the varied scope of their work, has been one of the most welcome developments of the era.

The recurring scenarios of the male-centred films and genres have occasionally been answered by 'female' equivalents. For example, the narrative of collective male endeavour is echoed by stories of self-empowerment in *School for Seduction*, *Calendar Girls* and *Rabbit Fever*, whilst *Women Talking Dirty* (1999), *Beautiful Creatures* (2000) and *High Heels and Low Lives* (2001) offer a glossily feminist spin on the 'buddy' movie, the gangster film and the caper movie.

However, there are some themes that distinguish the contemporary female-orientated films from their male counterparts. For example, the fixation with father-son bonds in the films discussed earlier is substituted for an interest in the complex dynamics of female relationships. In stories about close friendships such as *Career Girls*, *Me Without You* (2001), *Anita and Me*, *My Summer of Love*, *Gypo* and *Notes on a Scandal* there are sometimes homoerotic undercurrents, but the problematic relationships in these films are also a way to explore tensions and jealousies relating to age, gender, ethnic and intellectual difference.

As with many of the male films, there is a concern with 'performance' – the question of 'how to "do" femininity' (Brunsdon 2000: 167) – but with an emphasis on the role of the *voice*, either in written or oral form, rather than the body. British films have promoted and queried the female voice in varying ways. Although *Little Voice* accommodates the singing talents of its main star, Jane Horrocks, the film is ambivalent about her withdrawn young character's impersonations of female singers. A dreamer, like the characters of the similarly wistful *Janice Beard WPM* (1999) and *Very Annie Mary* (2001), with a domineering mother, she ultimately undergoes a sort of behavioural breakdown that is not dissimilar to that of Ray (Ray Winstone) in *Nil by Mouth*, someone else of many voices who constructs his identity through performance, and implodes when this is challenged. Despite being very different in tone, *Little Voice* makes for an interesting comparison with Lynne Ramsay's *Morvern Callar*, another story of a detached, unreadable young woman (played by Samantha Morton) who appropriates the 'voice' of others, in this case, a novel written and possibly even gifted to her by her dead boyfriend; Ramsay's enigmatic film refuses to define this act as theft, justice or self-liberation. In the realist melodrama *Stella Does Tricks* (1996), a teenage victim of abuse and prostitution (played by Kelly Macdonald) is last seen recounting her story to others, and therefore seizing control of her narrative for the first time. Other films, such as the historically-set *Vera Drake* and *Another Life*, work to give 'voice' to individuals, either real or imagined, who have been the victims of the prevailing attitudes of their time.

However, British cinema's best-known intervention within contemporary gender politics in recent years has most probably been the films based on Helen Fielding's bestselling *Bridget Jones* novels (the first published in 1996). Already a cultural phenomenon before the adaptations appeared, the thirtysomething Bridget Jones character (played by Renée Zellweger) became a hotly debated icon of post-feminism: on the one hand enjoying the lifestyle and professional career campaigned for by earlier waves of feminism, on the other hand in thrall to old-fashioned ideals of romantic courtship (see, for example, McRobbie 2007). Either way, the character articulated an aspect of contemporary experience that had rarely been addressed, and would go on to be a keynote work of 'chick-lit' fiction. Through their depiction of a woman experiencing both the freedom and loneliness of the 'singleton' existence, the books and films reflected the growing social trend for single-occupancy households. The first-person intimacy of the novels was carried across via the use of voice-over and inter-titles, but the films added further layers of self-reflexivity to an already densely intertextual creation through the casting of Colin Firth – who, in the role of Darcy in the BBC's *Pride and Prejudice*, was an object of lust for the literary Bridget – and also through the creative involvement of Richard Curtis and Hugh Grant, which connected the films to the cycle of romantic comedies set in an 'enchanted' London.

There has also been a loose cycle of films exploring behavioural responses to trauma and abuse. Films largely in the realist vein, such as *Stella Does Tricks*, *The War Zone*, *Hold Back the Night*, *Kidulthood* and *London to Brighton*, have dwelt upon the exploitation and sexual abuse of teenagers and young people, whilst *Afterlife*, *Girls' Night* (1998), *One More Kiss* (1999) and *Before You Go* (2002) are melodramatic films about the aftermath or end-stages of terminal illness.

However, some of the most fascinating statements about the complexity of sexual politics have been made by a group of female directors. Engaging with the interior lives of damaged young women, Carine Adler's *Under the Skin*, Lynne Ramsay's *Morvern Callar* and Andrea Arnold's *Red Road* draw provocative connections between emotional trauma – the death of loved ones – and sexual desire. All three filmmakers find cinematic ways (particularly editing) to express the intensity of their central character's grief, but also to render unclear their motivation and the extent of their passivity. In *Under the Skin*, which begins with the death of Iris's mother

Dangerous sexuality?: Jackie (Kate Dickie) plays voyeur in *Red Road*

from cancer, Iris (Samantha Morton) is rarely offscreen. As she embarks upon a series of humiliating sexual encounters, her thoughts are described through occasional voice-over. However, according to Charlotte Brunsdon, 'rather than allow Iris's voice-over to describe her loss, the film instead offers us the spectacle of Iris's self-degradation as her journey through her grief, showing us not sex as pleasure, but sex as a grief-torn attempt at both connection and obliteration, sex as the expression of pain and anger' (2000: 173).

Part revenge thriller, part commentary upon surveillance culture, *Red Road* is a generically intricate film about Jackie (Kate Dickie), an introverted, minimally-expressive council CCTV operator who sees onscreen the man who killed her husband and son in a car accident. By withholding information about this relationship between Jackie and Clyde (Tony Curran) until later in the narrative, the film finds a metaphor in the decoding of CCTV images for the viewer's own inability to read Jackie's subsequent flirtation with Clyde or to assess how her voyeurism affects the balance of power. The ambiguous representation of Jackie's pursuit of Clyde, which culminates in a graphic sex scene, was recognised as one of the film's strengths, but also caused some disquiet. Following their sexual encounter, Jackie has Clyde arrested for rape, although the film concludes with a scene of apparent mutual forgiveness. For Hannah McGill, 'the most intriguing aspect of *Red Road* is its refusal to define the degree to which Jackie's quest for vengeance is motivated by carnal curiosity' (2006: 27). But Lisa Mullen felt that Arnold had played 'dangerous games with the erotic aspect' of the relationship between the characters, and that the film dipped 'into the murky waters of rape fantasy' (2006: 78).

Albeit rarely to such controversial effect, the expression or containment of 'dangerous' female sexuality has been a recurring theme in contemporary British cinema, cropping up in films of differing genres and historical settings. In the 1950s-set drama *Asylum* (2005), Stella (Natasha Richardson), the wife of a prison officer, is punished twofold for her lust for a murderous inmate, becoming a social outcast but also a victim of her lover's pathological violence. Women are also penalised for their sexual desire in films such as *Another Life* and *The Mother*, or obliged to renounce it, as in *Mrs Brown* and *Elizabeth*.

Ethnicity

In her polemical survey of an uneasily multicultural Britain written at the turn of the century, Yasmin Alibhai-Brown accuses the British film industry of being 'myopic' in its failure to document and represent the experiences of ethnic minorities.

> It is not that they don't see us, but that filmmakers don't want us to litter up their olde world landscape. In this country 99 per cent of films are written by white, middle-class people for and about white middle-class people ... We have no Spike Lee yet or Denzel Washington because the much applauded film industry has done nothing to make them happen. (2001: 259)

These accusations are sweeping, but they encapsulate wider alarm about the perceived 'whiteness' of British film culture. Alibhai-Brown is not alone in singling out the films of Richard Curtis as particularly misrepresentative. In reference to *Notting Hill*, which makes no allusion to the capital's yearly carnival – a legendary expression of cultural diversity – she suggests that 'the producers, writers and directors could not have tried harder to whiten the most famously black area in London' (2001: 259). *The Full Monty*, another emblematical British comedy, similarly received criticism for the stereotyping of its one black character (played by Paul Barber) through his sexually-charged nickname, 'Horse' (see Alexander 2000: 113). The absence of non-white people in period dramas such as *Elizabeth* and *Shakespeare in Love* has also been taken as indicative of a general social and cultural silence about the 'historical presence in Britain of people of African or Caribbean descent' (Bourne 2002: 48).

Although these criticisms of UK film culture of the 1990s are compelling, they have slightly less application to the cinema of the 2000s, which has arguably been more receptive to the experience (and problems) of multicultural Britain. The perspectives of immigrants (past and present) have been acknowledged, for instance, in *Room to Rent* (2000), *Beautiful People*, *Dirty Pretty Things*, *Wondrous Oblivion* and *Brick Lane*, and filmmakers have been sensitive to the resulting clashes of culture, particularly the tensions between Muslim and white communities – as explored in *Yasmin*, *Love + Hate*, *Mischief Night* and elsewhere.

However, with regards to the most sizeable and deep-rooted communities of non-dominant ethnicity, an interesting schism becomes apparent when comparing the eminence of films by and about British Asians with those dealing with the experience of black Britons. A notable characteristic of contemporary black and Asian British filmmaking is its strategic targeting of a mainstream audience – in other words, a public that is not ethnically specific. In relation to this trend, Barbara Korte and Claudia Sternberg note:

A 'mainstreaming' of black and Asian British film has been observed in criticism and theory and articulated by an increasing number of practitioners themselves, referring to changing modes of production, distribution and reception and implying a more popular and commercial orientation of certain media products. (2004: 1)

But whilst a handful of British Asian films found commercial success, combining stories of ethnic specificity with universally palatable themes and situations, black British filmmaking has experienced some struggle in its 'bid for the mainstream', as Korte and Sternberg put it.

Indeed, the assimilation of British Asian narratives, characters and creative talent within UK film culture is one of the success stories of recent British cinema. This newfound confidence is apparent from the regional

A positive message: Jess (Parminder Nagra) and her football coach (Jonathan Rhys Meyers) in *Bend It Like Beckham*

and generic spread of representation, which encompasses historically-set films such as *East is East* and *Anita and Me*, comedies and more sobering dramas of culture-clash such as *Bend It Like Beckham, Bollywood Queen, Yasmin, My Son the Fanatic, Brick Lane* and *Ae Fond Kiss*, and films such as *Bride and Prejudice* (2005) and the cookery-based rom-com *Nina's Heavenly Delights*, which make no 'issue' of their stories of cross-cultural romance.

Even though problems of racism, and issues pertaining specifically to British Asian communities (such as arranged marriages and the impact of the 'war on terror') are often explored, the most populist films have stood accused of not being political enough, or sacrificing nuanced characterisation for a feelgood message. The director Gurinder Chadha, one of the leading figures of British Asian cinema, moved away from the didacticism of *Bhaji on the Beach* (1993), the film that had brought her and the screenwriter Meera Syal to prominence. Declaring herself 'tired with issue films' (quoted in Mather 2006: 189), but also mindful of the industrial climate, Chadha's subsequent projects *Bend It Like Beckham* and the Bollywood-flavoured *Bride and Prejudice* (a version of Jane Austen's similarly titled novel) were deliberately pitched at a broad audience. The message of *Bend It Like Beckham*, in particular, was taken as overwhelmingly positive, as the film 'confidently parallels the achievements of its British Asian heroine with the achievements of a white, English footballing hero, suggesting that Britain can now, perhaps, be perceived as a more integrated and unified community' (Mather 2006: 190). Being set within the specific *milieu* of London's Indian community gives texture to the story of Jess (Parminder Nagra) and her struggles to follow in the footsteps of David Beckham, but the filmmakers took care to make this a universally readable tale of teenage angst and gendered prejudice.

Although in some respects less visible, and perhaps because of this, black British cinema has tended to generate a more ardent – and often despairing – response. From June to November 2005, the British Film Institute ran a 'Black World' season, incorporating local and national screenings of black-themed cinema, DVD releases, educational projects and discussions. The season provided the opportunity for an evaluation of a black British cinema that could be traced back thirty years to pioneering and politicised films such as *Pressure* (1975), *Babylon* (1980) and *Burning an Illusion* (1981). Although the 1980s brought opportunities for the independent film sector, filmmakers of the 1990s with an interest in cultural politics had no option but to acclimatise themselves to market forces. *Young Soul Rebels* (1991), *Rage* (1999) and *Babymother* – all debut features by respected, academically-educated filmmakers – attempted to exploit the wider fascination with black British youth culture through a focus on musical performance. However, they made little commercial impact.

With a budget of £2 million, Julian Henriques' *Babymother* was the most expensive black British film yet made. Set exclusively among the council estates of Harlesden, North London, and featuring a mostly non-professional cast, the film tells the story of a teenage mother's struggle to become the 'queen' of the male-dominated local reggae and 'dancehall' community. The film garnered praise for its credible account of this vigorous and youthful subculture:

> This film is wired directly into the motor of assertive energy which is powering so-called multicultural Britain, to whose rhythm London is increasingly swinging. Indeed, dancehall represents the thin, shapely, aggressively stylised and eroticised black body of Hot Britain struggling to get out from inside the sleeker, fatter, complacent corporate figure of Cool Britannia. (Hall 1998: 26)

Without any significant white characters, and taking place beyond the dominant (white English) social structure, *Babymother* was open to accusations of evading issues of institutional discrimination, prejudice or racial tension. Yet, for Rachel Mosley-Wood, this allows for a focus on the 'Black subject as agent' (2004: 94). In its celebration of dancehall culture – which can ultimately be traced back to ancestral African roots – the film can be read as a subversive rejection of colonial power as an irrelevance to its West Indian immigrant descendents, who are allowed to proudly assert their 'primacy, relevance and significance at the site of the imperial culture ... which has historically relegated them to the margins and periphery' (2004: 91). Anita (Anjela Lauren Smith) and her 'rude girl' gang – who use Jamaican patois with a London accent – create a space for themselves that cannot be readily defined as either Caribbean or English but is nevertheless part of a redefinition of Britain as a multicultural society.

Following *Babymother*, it would be eight years before the appearance of any significant black-themed films. But the arrival of a cycle of London-based movies aimed once again at a youthful audience was not met with universal approval, with concern expressed about their lack of political ambition, negative stereotyping and narrow geographical focus.

Released at a time of escalating anxiety about gun and knife crime (not just in London but in cities such as Birmingham, Liverpool and Manchester), Saul Dibb's *Bullet Boy* exploited public awareness of its Hackney setting as the location for an infamous 'murder mile', an area synonymous with drug-related crime and gangland-style executions. The film gained a degree of authenticity – as well as marketability – through the casting of Ashley Walters, a pop star who had himself been jailed for the handling of a firearm, in the part of Ricky. While some critics and local residents praised the film's accuracy, others felt that it added to a body of regressive stereotypes about black men. For example, Joel Karamath felt that *Bullet Boy* offered a 'nihilistic and marginalised view of the world' (2007: 146) and Akin Ojumo was troubled by the 'fatalism' which drove its young characters to tragedy: 'what if the bullet boy becomes the defining image of young black masculinity?' (2005).

The series of 'urban' films that followed *Bullet Boy* – which included *Rollin' with the Nines* (2006), *Life and Lyrics* (2006) and *Kidulthood* – met with a similarly mixed reception. For some, they signalled the arrival of a market for an independent black cinema, offering a 'genuine insight into a world rarely documented for a wider audience' (Egere-Cooper 2006), and giving encouragement to nascent filmmakers (see Jaafar 2005). Some of the films were also praised for their documentation of musical developments, such as the uniquely British 'grime' scene (a hybrid of hip-hop and garage), as captured in *Rollin' with the Nines*.

But other commentators felt that the fetishisation of 'authenticity' in the production and discussion of black cinema ghettoised it within the genre of social realism. Tiring of the contemporary emphasis on gun crime and teenage delinquency, Ken Williams complained about the absence of 'stories of hope and the potential of our black youth', stressing that 'there are countless stories to be told about our communities and not all of them need to be firmly rooted in social realism to claim authenticity' (2006). Kevin Le Gendre also made the case for a cinema to reflect the plurality of the black British experience. Citing the lack of a 'black Harry Potter or Leroy Pottinger', he castigated the racism of the industry:

> Why should our children always have to sit through the urban grime of reality and not have some childhood fantasy? Why is this only left for middle-class white children? (2005)

Black British cinema was also deemed almost exclusively London-centric, as indeed it always had been. Amma Asante's *A Way of Life* – the story of Leigh-Anne (Stephanie James), a white teenage mother in South Wales who is responsible for the death of an Asian neighbour – was welcomed as a provincial alternative. Written and directed by a black Londoner, the film offered some hope for a 'colour-neutral' (ibid.) film culture, as well as scope for a looser definition of black British cinema.

Another area of contention was the inflection of black British cinema towards African-American models, with *Bullet Boy* deemed to be derivative of John Singleton's *Boyz N the Hood* (1991), and the rapping drama *Life and Lyrics* a local spin upon the Eminem vehicle *8 Mile* (2002), albeit with parochial references to British culture (such as catchphrases from the television comedy *Little Britain* (2003–)). At the same time, it could be argued that these films transcend racial categorisation to a certain degree, in that their characters are not solely defined by skin colour. For example, in *Bullet Boy*, Ricky's embarrassment at the prospect of being picked up from prison by his mother emphasises the universality of his adolescent rebelliousness. The moment in *Kidulthood* where a young black character, the hood-wearing Moony (Femi Oyeniran), rails against the taxi drivers who refuse to stop for him – 'Ain't that ironic – black cab don't take black man' – is a rare example of explicit political commentary in the otherwise de-politicised canon of contemporary urban cinema. By way of contrast, the sequence in *Life and Lyrics* in which a pair of dating characters take a touristic ride through the capital on an open-top bus functions to situate the film, and its characters, in the mainstream of British (film) culture, rather than proffering an ironic remark on their remoteness from it.

CONCLUSION

The preceding chapters have sketched the differing critical pathways that might be taken through the rich and varied terrain of contemporary British cinema. It is a testimony to this richness that this book has had to leave unaddressed some important lines of enquiry, from the input of particular screenwriters (such as Frank Cottrell Boyce or Peter Morgan), and of particular directors, to the extent to which films from different parts of the UK illuminate an understanding of regional identity. From its deployment of genre to its inter-relationship with other cultural forms, recent British cinema demands a diversity of enquiry to match the overwhelming heterogeneity of its output. Indeed, as innumerable film scholars have pointed out, it is this very quality that frustrates any attempt at overview or categorisation, let alone comprehension.

A consequence of this is the tendency to arrive at definitions of contemporary British cinema through its similarities and differences from the filmmaking of previous decades. For instance, Brian McFarlane's proposal that 'the more things change, the more some things at least stay the same' (2001: 273) is paralleled by Amy Sargeant's description of 'new wine in old bottles' (2005: 326). An analogous drive to understand British cinema through narrativising it – in other words, by identifying historical developments – can be located in critical work on how modern British films correspond with, or disrupt, traditional categories of genre.

An alternative approach places greater emphasis on how contemporary films chronicle and illuminate British lives, places and experiences in the new millennium. In his synoptic review of the reconstruction of British cultural identity since 1945, Peter Leese (2006) isolates three 'landmark' developments of political and social significance at the turn of the century:

> The effort to renew nationhood in the light of devolution; the attempt to leave behind the age of post-industrial 'lost certainties', especially by redevelopment and urban renewal; and the creation of a new imaginative consensus, a reworked version of the post-1945 'fair shares for all' ideal based on the model of multi-ethnic cultures. (2006: 175)

It is not difficult to locate examples of Blair-era films that engage with one or more of these developments, whether deliberately, unintentionally or with a degree of ambivalence. The close attention given by contemporary historians to the work of Gurinder Chadha, Richard Curtis, Ken Loach and others would seem to suggest that contemporary British cinema does have valuable things to say about issues of multiculturalism, national identity and industrial regeneration.

But a wholly academic approach leaves unaddressed the kind of questions that a lay viewer might pose about British film culture. Just how *good* is recent British cinema? How creative and resourceful are its practitioners? And how is it impacting upon hearts and minds domestically and worldwide?

As opposed to the scholarly endeavour of identifying relevance and historical coherence, the question of quality can only ever be answered subjectively. However, an indication of British cinema's marginalisation within international film culture is given by *Sight and Sound* magazine's poll of its contributors' favourite films of 2007. No British films made the top ten (James 2008: 5), although *This is England*, *Control* and *Eastern Promises* (2007) were mentioned in a handful of individual 'best of' lists.[1] Across critical and journalistic responses to recently released British films, it is not uncommon to observe unflattering comparisons with international filmmakers tackling similar material, making it quite possible to draw the conclusion that there are few works of British cinema that rival the intellectual rigour, storytelling confidence and creative achievement of non-UK films such as *Caché* (*Hidden*, 2005), *El Laberinto del fauno* (*Pan's Labyrinth*, 2006) and *Das Leben der Anderen* (*The Lives of Others*, 2006).

Disregarding any assessment of cinematic worth, it is theoretically possible to quantify the impact of contemporary British cinema through the extent to which various films and filmmakers have permeated the national consciousness and woven themselves into the cultural fabric of the nation. The most obvious contenders here, since 1997 at least, are *The Full Monty* and *Billy Elliot*, their stories, characters and production history almost taking on the status of modern-day myths, and their global reach extended by touring productions of stage musicals based on them. The achievement of these films is all the more remarkable for not being based on an audience's prior knowledge of a franchise, novel, advertisement,

The global face of British filmmaking?: Mr Bean (Rowan Atkinson) on his travels in *Mr Bean's Holiday*

A contemporary British icon?: Daniel Craig as 007 in *Casino Royale*

television programme, celebrity, legend or historical event, as is often the case for biopics, literary adaptations, comedies and period dramas. To a certain degree, British cinema has always drawn upon the nation's cultural and historical heritage, or from popular Hollywood genres; in this respect, contemporary filmmaking is no more or less parasitical than that of previous decades. Even *The Full Monty* and *Billy Elliot* draw from the familiar genre of British social realism as well as from theatrical traditions, and both make prominent use of internationally recognisable pop music on their soundtrack.

As for the global impact of British cinema, this can only ever be measured haphazardly, but two isolated examples from 2007 point to the paradoxical nature of its international eminence. In a year that saw the release of *Casino Royale* and *Mr Bean's Holiday*, there could surely be no two cultural ambassadors more different than James Bond (Daniel Craig) and Mr Bean (Rowan Atkinson), the former triggering worldwide discussion about contemporary Britishness as a result of the casting of a new 007, the latter cited in at least two political incidents. In November, an apparently floundering Prime Minister was ridiculed in the House of Commons for having changed from 'Stalin to Mr Bean'; in March that year, when Iranian warships seized Royal Navy personnel, one of the British crew reported that all he could understand during his 'terrifying' interrogation was the repeated mention of the hapless comic character (see Rumbelow 2007). The significance of Bond and Bean to the reputation of British cinema is another story, but given that these characters were established before 1997, the likelihood that they represent the global face of British filmmaking raises questions about whether the film culture of the Blair era has produced anything with such longevity and impact.

NOTES

chapter one

1   This information is sourced from the UK Film Council's website, which contains weekend nationwide box-office grosses for films released in UK cinemas; see http://www.ukfilmcouncil. org.uk/cinemagoing/boxoffice/ (accessed 1 January 2008).
2   This and subsequent data is taken from the UK Film Council's online Statistical Yearbook 2006–07; see http://www.ukfilmcouncil.org.uk/ information/statistics/yearbook/ (accessed 1 January 2008).
3   Information taken from the 'Qualifying as a British Film and Tax Relief' section of the UK Film Council's website; see http:// www.ukfilmcouncil. org.uk/filmmaking/filmingUK/taxreliefbritfilms/ (accessed 1 January 2008).

chapter two

1   Quotation taken from the Independent Film Parliament website; see http://www.filmparliament.org.uk/ (accessed 1 January 2008).

chapter three

1   These include lightweight capers like *You're Dead...* (1999) and *Fakers* (2004), the female-centred *Beautiful Creatures* (2000), the futuristic *24 Hours in London* (2000), films in the noir mode such as *Croupier* (1998), *Following*, *Puritan* and *Room 36* (2005), the car-thriller *Bodywork* (1999), the Shakespeare-inspired *My Kingdom*, revenge thrillers such as *The Late Twentieth* (2002), *The Revengers Tragedy* and *I'll Sleep*

When I'm Dead (2003), the films stylising themselves like contemporary westerns such as *Dead Man's Cards*, and the one-of-a-kind *Man Dancin'* (2003) in which a reformed hardman puts his energies into the staging of a community passion play.

2   Examples of the sex comedies and television spin-offs that arguably characterise the output of the British film industry in the 1970s include *Confessions of a Window Cleaner* (1974), *Percy's Progress* (1974), *On the Buses* (1971) and *The Likely Lads* (1976).

3   Overviews of the 'heritage debate' are plentiful; see, for example, Hall (2001); Monk (2002); Dave (2006: 27–44).

4   Examples of iconoclastic or 'inauthentic' takes on history in British film culture include *Carry On Henry* (1971), *Lisztomania* (1975), *The Draughtsman's Contract* (1982) and *Caravaggio* (1986).

chapter four

1   Newcastle United and St James's Park also feature prominently in the 'rags-to-riches' soccer fantasy *Goal!* (2005). In this film the importance of football to the regional culture is alluded to, but rendered insignificant by the narrative focus on the rapid rise of a teenager from the slums of South America to become the team's star player; the local 'underclass' is consequently removed from the picture.

2   The term 'chav' is a (mostly) derogatory slang term for the fashions and lifestyle of some members of the British working class. The term had entered popular parlance and mainstream dictionaries by 2005, although it had been in circulation for some time prior to that, in differing forms.

conclusion

1   For a full list of films cited in the *Sight and Sound* 2007 poll see http://www.bfi.org.uk/sightandsound/pdf/films-of-the-year-2007.pdf (accessed 1 January 2008).

FILMOGRAPHY

Unless stated otherwise, all films listed are UK productions. Information about release date and country/countries of origin is taken from the Internet Movie Database (http://www.imdb.com). UK-set and/or English-language co-productions with non-English speaking countries are given by their English title.

8 Mile (Curtis Hanson, 2002, USA/Germany)
11'09"01 – September 11 (Youssef Chahine *et al.*, 2002, UK/Egypt/France/
    Iran/Japan/Mexio/USA)
51st State, The (Ronny Yu, 2001, UK/Canada)
9 Dead Gay Guys (Lab Ky Mo, 2002)
9 Songs (Michael Winterbottom, 2004)
16 Years of Alcohol (Richard Jobson, 2003)
33x Around the Sun (John Hardwick, 2005)
28 Days Later (Danny Boyle, 2002)
28 Weeks Later (Juan Carlos Fresnadillo, 2007, UK/Spain)
24 Hour Party People (Michael Winterbottom, 2002)
24 Hours in London (Alexander Finbow, 2000)
2001: A Space Odyssey (Stanley Kubrick, 1968, UK/USA)
A Clockwork Orange (Stanley Kubrick, 1971)
A Cock and Bull Story (Michael Winterbottom, 2005)
A Room for Romeo Brass (Shane Meadows, 1999, UK/Canada)
A Room with a View (James Ivory, 1985)
A Way of Life (Amma Asante, 2004)
About a Boy (Chris and Paul Weitz, 2002, UK/USA/France/Germany)
Ae Fond Kiss (Ken Loach, 2004, UK/Belgium/Germany/Italy/Spain)
Afterlife (Alison Peebles, 2003)
AKA (Duncan Roy, 2002)

Alien (Ridley Scott, 1979, UK/USA)
Alien Autopsy (Jonny Campbell, 2006, UK/Germany)
Ali G Indahouse (Mark Mylod, 2002)
All or Nothing (Mike Leigh, 2002, UK/France)
Alpha Male (Dan Wilde, 2006, UK/USA)
Amy Foster (Beeban Kidron, 1997, UK/Canada/USA)
An Ideal Husband (Oliver Parker, 1999, UK/USA)
Analyze This (Harold Ramis, 1999, USA/Australia)
And When Did You Last See Your Father? (Anand Tucker, 2007, UK/Ireland)
Angus, Thongs and Perfect Snogging (Gurinder Chadha, 2008, USA)
Anita and Me (Metin Hüseyin, 2002)
Another Life (Philip Goodhew, 2001)
Asylum (David Mackenzie, 2005, UK/Ireland)
Atonement (Joe Wright, 2007, UK/France)
Avengers, The (Jeremiah S. Chechik, 1998, USA)
Babylon (Franco Roso, 1980, UK/Italy)
Babymother (Julian Henriques, 1998)
Bean (Mel Smith, 1997, UK/USA)
Beautiful Creatures (Bill Eagles, 2000)
Beautiful People (Jasmin Dizdar, 1999)
Beautiful Thing (Hettie MacDonald, 1996)
Becoming Jane (Julian Jarrold, 2007)
Bedrooms and Hallways (Rose Troche, 1998)
Before You Go (Lewis Gilbert, 2002)
Beginner's Luck (James Callis and Nick Cohen, 2001)
Bend It Like Beckham (Gurinder Chadha, 2002, UK/Germany/USA)
Beowulf (Robert Zemeckis, 2007, USA)
Bhaji on the Beach (Gurinder Chadha, 1993)
Big Tease, The (Kevin Allen, 1999, UK/USA)
Billy Elliot (Stephen Daldry, 2000)
Blackball (Mel Smith, 2003)
Bleak Moments (Mike Leigh, 1971)
Blinded (Eleanor Yule, 2004)
Bloody Sunday (Paul Greengrass, 2002, UK/Ireland)
Bodysong (Simon Pummell, 2003)
Bodywork (Gareth Rhys Jones, 1999)
Bollywood Queen (Jeremy Wooding, 2002)

Borat: Cultural Learnings of America for Make Benefit Glorious Nation of Kazakhstan (Larry Charles, 2006, USA)

Born Romantic (David Kane, 2000)

Boy Eats Girl (Stephen Bradley, 2005, UK/Ireland)

Boyz N the Hood (John Singleton, 1991, USA)

Brassed Off (Mark Herman, 1996, UK/USA)

Bread and Roses (Ken Loach, 2000, UK/France/Germany/Italy/ Switzerland)

Breaking and Entering (Anthony Minghella, 2006, UK/USA)

Breaking the Waves (Lars von Trier, 1996, Denmark/Sweden/France/ Netherlands/Norway/Iceland)

Brick Lane (Sarah Gavron, 2007)

Bride and Prejudice (Gurinder Chadha, 2005, UK/USA)

Brideshead Revisited (Julian Jarrold, 2008, UK)

Bridget Jones's Diary (Sharon Maguire, 2001, UK/France)

Bridget Jones: The Edge of Reason (Beeban Kidron, 2004, UK/France/Germany/Ireland/USA)

Bright Young Things (Stephen Fry, 2003)

Brothers of the Head (Keith Fulton and Louis Pepe, 2005)

Bullet Boy (Saul Dibb, 2004)

Bunker, The (Rob Green, 2001)

Burning an Illusion (Menelik Shabazz, 1981)

Business, The (Nick Love, 2005, UK/Spain)

Caché (Hidden) (Michael Haneke, 2005, Austria/France/Germany/Italy)

Calcium Kid, The (Alex De Rakoff, 2004)

Calendar Girls (Nigel Cole, 2003, UK/USA)

Calvaire (The Ordeal) (Fabrice Du Welz, 2004, Belgium/France/ Luxembourg)

Career Girls (Mike Leigh, 1997, UK/France)

Carla's Song (Ken Loach, 1995, UK/Germany/Spain)

Casino Royale (Martin Campbell, 2006, UK/USA/Germany/Czech Republic)

Changeling, The (Marcus Thompson, 1998)

Chariots of Fire (Hugh Hudson, 1981)

Charlie and the Chocolate Factory (Tim Burton, 2005, UK/USA)

Charlotte Gray (Gillian Armstrong, 2001, UK/Australia/Germany)

Chicken Run (Peter Lord and Nick Park, 2000)

Chicken Tikka Masala (Harmage Singh Kalirai, 2005)

Children of Men (Alfonso Cuarón, 2006, UK/USA/Japan)

Children's Midsummer Night's Dream, The (Christine Edzard, 2001)

Christie Malry's Own Double-Entry (Paul Tickell, 2000, UK/Luxembourg/ Netherlands)

Chronicles of Narnia, The: The Lion, the Witch and the Wardrobe (Andrew Adamson, 2005, USA)

Chunky Monkey (Greg Cruttwell, 2003)

Churchill: The Hollywood Years (Peter Richardson, 2004)

Circus (Rob Walker, 2000, UK/USA)

Claim, The (Michael Winterbottom, 2000, UK/Canada/France)

Closer (Mike Nichols, 2004, USA)

Code 46 (Michael Winterbottom, 2003)

Confetti (Debbie Isitt, 2006)

Constant Gardener, The (Fernando Meirelles, 2005, UK/Germany)

Control (Anton Corbijn, 2007, UK/USA/Australia/Japan)

Cradle of Fear (Alex Chandon, 2001)

Creep (Christopher Smith, 2004, UK/Germany)

Croupier (Mike Hodges, 1998, UK/France/Germany/Ireland)

Curse of Frankenstein, The (Terence Fisher, 1957)

Dark, The (John Fawcett, 2005, UK/Germany)

Darkest Light, The (Simon Beaufoy and Billie Eltringham, 1999, UK/ France)

Das Leben der Anderen (*The Lives of Others*) (Florian Henckel von Donnersmarck, 2006, Germany)

Da Vinci Code, The (Ron Howard, 2006, USA)

Dead Man's Cards (James Marquand, 2006)

Dead Man's Shoes (Shane Meadows, 2004)

Dear Frankie (Shona Auerbach, 2004)

Deathwatch (Michael J. Bassett, 2002, UK/Germany)

Den Eneste Ene (*The One and Only*) (Susanne Bier, 1999, Denmark)

Descent, The (Neil Marshall, 2005)

Different for Girls (Richard Spence, 1996, UK/France)

Dirty Pretty Things (Stephen Frears, 2002)

Dirty Sanchez: The Movie (Jim Hickey, 2006)

Dog Soldiers (Neil Marshall, 2002, UK/Luxembourg)

Do I Love You? (Lisa Gornick, 2002)

Downtime (Bharat Nalluri, 1997, UK/France)
Duchess, The (Saul Dibb, 2008, UK/USA/Denmark)
Eastern Promises (David Cronenberg, 2007, UK/Canada/USA)
East is East (Damien O'Donnell, 1999)
Eden Lake (James Watkins, 2008)
Elizabeth (Shekhar Kapur, 1998)
Elizabeth: The Golden Age (Shekhar Kapur, 2007, UK/France/Germany)
End of the Affair, The (Neil Jordan, 1999, UK/USA)
Enduring Love (Roger Michell, 2004)
English Patient, The (Anthony Minghella, 1996, USA)
Enigma (Michael Apted, 2001, UK/USA/Germany/Netherlands)
Everything (Richard Hawkins, 2004)
Evil Aliens (Jake West, 2005)
Exodus (Penny Woolcock, 2007)
Face (Antonia Bird, 1997)
Fakers (Richard Janes, 2004)
Fanny and Elvis (Kay Mellor, 1999)
Fargo (Joel Coen, 1996, USA)
Felicia's Journey (Atom Egoyan, 1999, UK/Canada)
Festen (*The Celebration*) (Thomas Vinterberg, 1998, Denmark/Sweden)
Festival (Annie Griffin, 2005)
Fever Pitch (David Evans, 1997)
Filth and the Fury, The (Julien Temple, 2000, UK/USA)
Finding Neverland (Marc Forster, 2004, UK/USA)
Following (Christopher Nolan, 1998)
Football Factory, The (Nick Love, 2004)
Four Weddings and a Funeral (Mike Newell, 1994)
Freeze Frame (John Simpson, 2004, UK/Ireland)
From Hell (Albert and Allen Hughes, 2001, USA)
Frozen (Juliet McKoen, 2005)
Full Monty, The (Peter Cattaneo, 1997)
Gabriel and Me (Udayan Prasad, 2001)
Gallivant (Andrew Kötting, 1997)
Gangster No. 1 (Paul McGuigan, 2000, UK/Germany/Ireland)
Get Carter (Mike Hodges, 1971)
Get Real (Simon Shore, 1998)
Ghosts (Nick Broomfield, 2006)

Gigolos, The (Richard Bracewell, 2006)

Girls' Night (Nick Hurran, 1998)

Goal! (Danny Cannon, 2005, UK/USA)

Going Off Big Time (Jim Doyle, 2000)

Golden Bowl, The (James Ivory, 2000, UK/France/USA)

Golden Compass, The (Chris Weitz, 2007, UK/USA)

Goodbye Charlie Bright (Nick Love, 2001)

Gosford Park (Robert Altman, 2001, UK/Italy/USA)

Government Inspector, The (Peter Kosminksy, 2005)

Great Ecstasy of Robert Carmichael, The (Thomas Clay, 2005)

Greenfingers (Joel Hershman, 2000, UK/USA)

Green Street (Levi Alexander, 2004, UK/USA)

Gregory's Two Girls (Bill Forsyth, 1999, UK/Germany)

Greyfriars Bobby (John Henderson, 2005)

Grow Your Own (Richard Laxton, 2007)

Guest House Paradiso (Adrian Edmondson, 1999)

Gypo (Jan Dunn, 2005)

Hallam Foe (David Mackenzie, 2007)

Hamlet (Michael Almereyda, 2000, USA)

Hardware (Richard Stanley, 1990)

Harry Potter and the Chamber of Secrets (Chris Columbus, 2002, UK/Germany/USA)

Harry Potter and the Goblet of Fire (Mike Newell, 2005, UK/USA)

Harry Potter and the Order of the Phoenix (David Yates, 2007, UK/USA)

Harry Potter and the Philosopher's Stone (Chris Columbus, 2001, UK/USA)

Harry Potter and the Prisoner of Azkaban (Alfonso Cuarón, 2004, UK/USA)

Haute tension (*Switchblade Romance*) (Alexandre Aja, 2003, France)

Heartlands (Damien O'Donnell, 2002, UK/USA)

Hellraiser (Clive Barker, 1987)

Heroes and Villains (Selwyn Roberts, 2006)

High Heels and Low Lifes (Mel Smith, 2001, UK/USA)

Hilary and Jackie (Anand Tucker, 1998)

History Boys, The (Nicholas Hytner, 2006)

Hold Back the Night (Philip Davies, 1999)

Hole, The (Nick Hamm, 2001)

Hope and Glory (John Boorman, 1987)

Hotel (Mike Figgis, 2001, UK/Italy)

Hot Fuzz (Edgar Wright, 2007, UK/France)

House! (Julian Kemp, 2000)

House of Mirth, The (Terence Davies, 2000, UK/USA)

Howards End (James Ivory, 1992, UK/Japan)

Human Traffic (Justin Kerrigan, 1999, UK/Ireland)

I'll Be There (Craig Ferguson, 2003, UK/USA)

I'll Sleep When I'm Dead (Mike Hodges, 2003, UK/USA)

Imagine Me and You (Ol Parker, 2005, UK/USA/Germany)

Importance of Being Earnest, The (Oliver Parker, 2002, UK/USA)

In This World (Michael Winterbottom, 2002)

Intimacy (Patrice Chéreau, 2001, UK/France/Germany/Spain)

In Which We Serve (Noel Coward and David Lean, 1942)

Iris (Richard Eyre, 2001, UK/USA)

Italian Job, The (Peter Collinson, 1969)

It's a Free World... (Ken Loach, 2007, UK/Italy/Germany/Spain)

It's All Gone Pete Tong (Michael Dowse, 2004, UK/Canada)

I Want Candy (Stephen Surjik, 2007)

Janice Beard 45 WPM (Clare Kilner, 1999)

Jealous God, The (Steven Woodcock, 2005)

Joe Strummer: The Future is Unwritten (Julien Temple, 2007)

Jude (Michael Winterbottom, 1996)

Julie and the Cadillacs (Bryan Izzard, 1999)

Julien Donkey-Boy (Harmony Korine, 1999, USA)

Keep the Aspidistra Flying (Robert Bierman, 1997)

Kes (Ken Loach, 1969)

Kevin & Perry Go Large (Ed Bye, 2000, UK/USA)

Kidulthood (Menhaj Huda, 2006)

Killing of John Lennon, The (Andrew Piddington, 2006)

Kind of Hush, A (Brian Stirner, 1999)

King Arthur (Antoine Fuqua, 2004, UK/Ireland/USA)

King is Alive, The (Kristian Levring, 2001, Denmark/Sweden/USA)

Kinky Boots (Julian Jarrold, 2005, UK/USA)

Kiss of Life (Emily Young, 2003, UK/France)

Laberinto del fauno, El (*Pan's Labyrinth*) (Guillermo del Toro, 2006, Mexico/Spain/USA)

Ladies in Lavender (Charles Dance, 2004)

Land and Freedom (Ken Loach, 1995, UK/Spain/Germany/Italy)

Land Girls, The (David Leland, 1998, UK/France)
Large (Justin Edgar, 2001)
Lassie (Charles Sturridge, 2005, UK/France/Ireland/USA)
Last Great Wilderness, The (David Mackenzie, 2002, UK/Denmark)
Last Horror Movie, The (Julian Richards, 2003)
Last King of Scotland, The (Kevin Macdonald, 2006)
Last Orders (Fred Schepsi, 2001, UK/Germany)
Last Resort (Pawel Pawlikowski, 2000)
Late Twentieth (Hadi Hajaig, 2002)
Lawless Heart, The (Tom Hunsinger and Neil Hunter, 2001, UK/France)
Layer Cake (Matthew Vaughn, 2004)
League of Gentlemen's Apocalypse, The (Steve Bendelack, 2005, UK/
    Ireland/USA)
Liam (Stephen Frears, 2000, UK/France/Germany)
Life and Lyrics (Richard Laxton, 2006)
Lighthouse (Simon Hunter, 2000)
Like Father (Amber, 2001)
Little Voice (Mark Herman, 1997)
Lives of the Saints, The (Chris Cottam and Rankin, 2006)
Local Hero (Bill Forsyth, 1983)
Lock, Stock and Two Smoking Barrels (Guy Ritchie, 1998)
London (Patrick Keiller, 1994)
London to Brighton (Paul Andrew Williams, 2006)
Long Good Friday, The (John Mackenzie, 1980)
Lord of the Rings, The: The Fellowship of the Ring (Peter Jackson, 2001,
    USA/New Zealand)
Lord of the Rings, The: The Return of the King (Peter Jackson, 2003, USA/
    New Zealand/Germany)
Lord of the Rings, The: The Two Towers (Peter Jackson, 2002, USA/
    Germany/New Zealand)
Lost Son, The (Chris Menges, 1999, France/UK/USA)
Love Actually (Richard Curtis, 2003, UK/USA)
Love and Death on Long Island (Richard Kwietniowski, 1997, UK/Canada)
Love + Hate (Dominic Savage, 2005, UK/Ireland)
Love, Honour and Obey (Dominic Anciano and Ray Burdis, 2000)
Love is the Devil (John Maybury, 1998, UK/France/Japan)
Love's Labour's Lost (Kenneth Branagh, 2000, UK/Canada/France)

Low Down, The (Jamie Thraves, 2000)

Lucky Break (Peter Cattaneo, 2001, UK/Germany)

Mad Cows (Sara Sugarman, 1999)

Magicians (Andrew O'Connor, 2007)

Man Dancin' (Norman Stone, 2003)

Mansfield Park (Patricia Rozema, 1999)

Mark of Cain, The (Marc Munden, 2007)

Married/Unmarried (Noli, 2001)

Martha, Meet Daniel, Frank and Laurence (Nick Hamm, 1998)

Match, The (Mick Davis, 1999)

Match Point (Woody Allen, 2005, UK/USA/Luxembourg)

Maurice (James Ivory, 1987)

Mauvais passe (*The Escort*) (Michel Blanc, 1999, France)

Mean Machine (Barry Skolnick, 2001, UK/USA)

Merchant of Venice, The (Michael Radford, 2004, UK/Italy/Luxembourg/
   USA)

Me Without You (Sandra Goldbacher, 2001, UK/Germany)

Mike Bassett England Manager (Steve Barron, 2001, UK/USA)

Millions (Danny Boyle, 2004, UK/USA)

MirrorMask (Dave McKean, 2004, UK/USA)

Mischief Night (Penny Woolcock, 2006)

Miss Potter (Chris Noonan, 2006, UK/USA)

Mojo (Jez Butterworth, 1997)

Morvern Callar (Lynne Ramsay, 2002)

Mother, The (Roger Michell, 2003)

Mr Bean's Holiday (Steve Bendelack, 2007, UK/France/Germany/USA)

Mr In-Between (Paul Sarossy, 2001)

Mrs Brown (John Madden, 1997, UK/Ireland/USA)

Mrs Caldicot's Cabbage War (Ian Sharp, 2000)

Mrs Dalloway (Marleen Gorris, 1997, UK/USA/Netherlands)

Mrs Henderson Presents (Stephen Frears, 2005)

My Beautiful Laundrette (Stephen Frears, 1985)

My Brother Tom (Dom Rotheroe, 2001)

My Kingdom (Don Boyd, 2001, UK/Italy)

My Little Eye (Marc Evans, 2002, UK/USA/France/Canada)

My Name is Joe (Ken Loach, 1998, UK/France/Germany/Italy/Spain)

My Son the Fanatic (Udayan Prasad, 1997, UK/France)

My Summer of Love (Pawel Pawlikowski, 2004)
Nanny McPhee (Kirk Jones, 2005, UK/USA/France)
Nasty Neighbours (Debbie Isitt, 2000)
Navigators, The (Ken Loach, 2001, UK/Spain/Italy/France)
Nicholas Nickleby (Douglas McGrath, 2002, UK/USA/Germany/
    Netherlands)
Nil by Mouth (Gary Oldman, 1997, UK/France)
Nina's Heavenly Delights (Pratibha Parmar, 2006)
Nine Lives of Tomas Katz, The (Ben Hopkins, 2000, UK/Germany)
Notes on a Scandal (Richard Eyre, 2006)
Notting Hill (Roger Michell, 1999, UK/USA)
O (Tim Blake Nelson, 2001, USA)
Of Time and the City (Terence Davies, 2008)
Oliver Twist (Roman Polanski, 2005, UK/France/Czech Republic)
Omagh (Pete Travis, 2004, UK/Ireland)
Omen, The (Richard Donner, 1976, UK/USA)
On a Clear Day (Gaby Dellal, 2005)
Once Upon a Time in the Midlands (Shane Meadows, 2002, UK/Germany)
One and Only, The (Simon Cellan Jones, 2002, UK/France)
One Day in September (Kevin Macdonald, 1999, UK/Germany/
    Switzerland)
One for the Road (Chris Cooke, 2003, UK/USA)
One Last Chance (Stewart Svaasand, 2004, UK/Norway)
One More Kiss (Vadim Jean, 1999)
Orphans (Peter Mullan, 1997)
Oscar and Lucinda (Gillian Armstrong, 1997, UK/Australia/USA)
Outlaw (Nick Love, 2007)
Out of Depth (Simon Marshall, 2000)
Pandaemonium (Julien Temple, 2000)
Parole Officer, The (John Duigan, 2001)
Performance (Donald Cammell and Nicolas Roeg, 1970)
Pervirella (Alex Chandon and Josh Collins, 1997)
Peter Pan (P. J. Hogan, 2003, USA/UK)
Phantom of the Opera, The (Joel Schumacher, 2004, UK/USA)
Pierrepoint (Adrian Shergold, 2005)
Plague, The (Greg Hall, 2006)
Portrait of a Lady, The (Jane Campion, 1996, UK/USA)

Possession (Neil LaBute, 2002, UK/USA)

Preaching to the Perverted (Stuart Urban, 1997)

Pressure (Horace Ové, 1976)

Pretty Woman (Garry Marshall, 1990, USA)

Prick Up Your Ears (Stephen Frears, 1987)

Pride and Prejudice (Joe Wright, 2005, UK/France)

Principles of Lust, The (Penny Woolcock, 2003)

Private Life of Henry VIII, The (Alexander Korda, 1936)

Pure (Gillies MacKinnon, 2002)

Purely Belter (Mark Herman, 2000)

Puritan (Hadi Hajaig, 2005)

Queen, The (Stephen Frears, 2006, UK/France/Italy)

Rabbit Fever (Ian Denyer, 2006)

Rage (Newton Aduaka, 1999, UK/Nigeria)

Raining Stones (Ken Loach, 1993)

Rancid Aluminium (Edward Thomas, 2000)

Ratcatcher (Lynne Ramsay, 1999, UK/France)

Rave Macbeth (Klaus Knoesel, 2001, Germany)

Razor Blade Smile (Jake West, 1998)

Red Road (Andrea Arnold, 2006, UK/Denmark)

Remains of the Day (James Ivory, 1993, UK/USA)

Revengers Tragedy, The (Alex Cox, 2002)

Revolver (Guy Ritchie, 2005, UK/France)

Riff Raff (Ken Loach, 1990)

Ringu (*Ring*) (Hideo Nakata, 1998, Japan)

Road to Guantánamo, The (Mat Whitecross and Michael Winterbottom, 2006)

Robinson in Space (Patrick Keiller, 1997)

Rocket Post, The (Stephen Whittaker, 2004)

RocknRolla (Guy Ritchie, 2008)

Rollin' with the Nines (Julian Gilbey, 2006)

Romeo + Juliet (Baz Luhrmann, 1996, USA)

Room 36 (Jim Groom, 2002)

Room to Rent (Khalid El Hagar, 2000, UK/France)

Run, Fat Boy, Run (David Schwimmer, 2007, UK/USA)

Sacred Flesh (Nigel Wingrove, 2000)

Saint, The (Phillip Noyce, 1997, USA)

Saving Grace (Nigel Cole, 2000)
Scarlet Tunic, The (Stuart St. Paul, 1998)
Scenes of a Sexual Nature (Ed Blum, 2006)
School for Seduction (Sue Heel, 2004)
S Club: Seeing Double (Nigel Dick, 2003)
Secret Agent, The (Christopher Hampton, 1996)
Secrets and Lies (Mike Leigh, 2006, UK/France)
Severance (Christopher Smith, 2006, UK/Germany)
Sex Lives of the Potato Men (Andy Humphries, 2004)
Sexy Beast (Jonathan Glazer, 2000, UK/Spain/USA)
Shadowlands (Richard Attenborough, 1993)
Shakespeare in Love (John Madden, 1998, UK/USA)
Shaun of the Dead (Edgar Wright, 2004, UK/France)
Shining, The (Stanley Kubrick, 1980, UK/USA)
Shooting Magpies (Amber, 2005)
Simon Magus (Ben Hopkins, 1999, UK/France/Germany/Italy/USA)
Sixty Six (Paul Weiland, 2006)
Sleuth (Kenneth Branagh, 2007, USA)
Sliding Doors (Peter Howitt, 1998, UK/USA)
Small Time (Shane Meadows, 1996)
Small Time Obsession (Piotr Szkopiak, 2000)
Snatch (Guy Ritchie, 2000, UK/USA)
Solaris (Andrei Tarkovsky, 1972, Soviet Union)
Somers Town (Shane Meadows, 2008)
Son of Rambow (Garth Jennings, 2007, UK/France/Germany)
Song of Songs (Josh Appignanesi, 2006)
Sorted (Alexander Jovy, 2000, UK/USA)
South West Nine (Richard Parry, 2001, UK/Ireland)
Spice World (Bob Spiers, 1997)
Spider (David Cronenberg, 2002, UK/France/Canada)
Spirit Trap (David Smith, 2005, UK)
Stage Beauty (Richard Eyre, 2004, UK/Germany/USA)
Stella Does Tricks (Coky Giedroyc, 1996)
Still Crazy (Brian Gibson, 1998)
Stoned (Stephen Woolley, 2005)
Stormbreaker (Geoffrey Sax, 2006, UK/Germany/USA)
Straightheads (Dan Reed, 2007, UK)

Straw Dogs (Sam Peckinpah, 1971, UK/USA)

Strictly Sinatra (Peter Capaldi, 2001)

St Trinian's (Oliver Parker and Barnaby Thompson, 2007)

Sunshine (Danny Boyle, 2007, UK/USA)

Sweeney Todd: The Demon Barber of Fleet Street (Tim Burton, 2007, UK/USA)

Sweet Sixteen (Ken Loach, 2002, UK/Germany/Spain)

Sylvia (Christine Jeffs, 2003)

There's Only One Jimmy Grimble (John Hay, 2000, UK/France)

These Foolish Things (Julia Taylor-Stanley, 2006)

This Filthy Earth (Andrew Kötting, 2001)

This is England (Shane Meadows, 2006)

This Year's Love (David Kane, 1999)

Thunderpants (Peter Hewitt, 2002, UK/France/Germany/Italy/Netherlands/USA)

Tichborne Claimant, The (David Yates, 1998)

Tickets (Abbas Kiarostami, Ken Loach and Ermanno Olmi, 2005, UK/Italy)

Timecode (Mike Figgis, 2000, USA)

Titus (Julie Taymor, 1999, UK/USA)

To Kill a King (Mike Barker, 2003, UK/Germany)

Tomorrow La Scala! (Francesca Joseph, 2002)

Top Spot (Tracey Emin, 2004)

Topsy-Turvy (Mike Leigh, 1999)

Touching the Void (Kevin Macdonald, 2003)

Trainspotting (Danny Boyle, 1996)

Trauma (Marc Evans, 2004)

Truth About Love, The (John Hay, 2004)

Twenty Four Seven (Shane Meadows, 1997)

Two Men Went to War (John Henderson, 2002)

Underground (Paul Spurrier, 1998)

Under the Skin (Carine Adler, 1997)

United 93 (Paul Greengrass, 2006, UK/France/USA)

Unleashed (Louis Leterrier, 2005, UK/France/USA)

Urban Ghost Story (Geneviève Jolliffe, 1998)

Valiant (Gary Chapman, 2005)

Vanity Fair (Mira Nair, 2004, UK/USA)

Velvet Goldmine (Todd Haynes, 1998, UK/USA)

Venus (Roger Michell, 2006)

Vera Drake (Mike Leigh, 2004, UK/France/New Zealand)

Very Annie Mary (Sara Sugarman, 2001, UK/France)

V for Vendetta (James McTeigue, 2005, USA/UK/Germany)

Wah-Wah (Richard E. Grant, 2005, UK/France/South Africa)

Wallace and Gromit: The Curse of the Were-Rabbit (Steve Box and Nick Park, 2005)

Warrior, The (Aisf Kapadia, 2001, UK/France/Germany)

War Bride, The (Lyndon Chubbuck, 2001, UK/Canada)

War Zone, The (Tim Roth, 1999, UK/Italy)

Whisky Galore (Alexander Mackendrick, 1949)

Wicker Man, The (Robin Hardy, 1973)

Wilbur Wants to Kill Himself (Lone Scherfig, 2002, UK/Denmark/Sweden/ France)

Wild Country (Craig Strachan, 2005)

Wilde (Brian Gilbert, 1997, UK/Germany/Japan)

Wilderness (Michael J. Bassett, 2006)

Wimbledon (Richard Loncraine, 2004, UK/France)

Wind That Shakes the Barley, The (Ken Loach, 2006, UK/Ireland/ Germany/Italy/Spain/France)

Wings of the Dove, The (Iain Softley, 1997, UK/USA)

Winslow Boy, The (David Mamet, 1999, UK/USA)

Women Talking Dirty (Coky Giedroyc, 1999)

Wonderland (Michael Winterbottom, 1999)

Wondrous Oblivion (Paul Morrison, 2003, UK/Germany)

Woodlanders, The (Phil Agland, 1997)

Yasmin (Simon Beaufoy, 2004, UK/Germany)

Yes (Sally Potter, 2004, UK/USA)

Young Adam (David Mackenzie, 2003, UK/France)

Young Soul Rebels (Isaac Julien, 1991, UK/France/Germany/Spain)

You're Dead... (Andy Hurst, 1999, UK/Germany/USA)

Television programmes/series

The network and date of first transmission are listed. One-off television dramas are listed in the Filmography.

Blackadder (BBC, 1983)
Bleak House (BBC, 2005)
Book Group, The (Channel Four, 2002)
Coronation Street (ITV, 1960)
Days of Hope (BBC, 1975)
Doctor Who (BBC, 1963; relaunched 2005)
Elizabeth I (BBC, 2005)
Life on Mars (BBC, 2006)
Little Britain (BBC, 2003)
Mr Bean (ITV, 1990)
Nighty Night (BBC, 2004)
Office, The (BBC, 2001)
Pride and Prejudice (BBC, 1995)
Royle Family, The (BBC, 1998)
Shameless (Channel Four, 2004)
Sopranos, *The* (HBO, 1999)
Spaced (Channel Four, 1999)
Tipping the Velvet (BBC, 2002)
Virgin Queen (Channel Four, 2005)
Who Do You Think You Are? (BBC, 2004)
Young Ones, The (BBC, 1982)

BIBLIOGRAPHY

The bibliography lists works cited in the text and is also designed to point to further reading. The annotated list of 'essential reading' highlights work that will provide a useful and comprehensive introduction to the study of contemporary British cinema, although many valuable contributions are also to be found under 'secondary reading'. However, as critical material is still emerging, it is certain that these will be supplemented by new scholarship of equal value.

Essential Reading

In addition to the works listed below, the *Journal of British Cinema and Television*, *Screen* and *Sight and Sound* are worth consulting for coverage of recent British film culture.

Ashby, J. and A. Higson (eds) (2000) *British Cinema, Past and Present*. London and New York: Routledge.
This anthology contains an indispensable section on contemporary British cinema.
Blandford, S. (2007) *Film, Drama and the Break-up of Britain*. Bristol and Chicago: Intellect.
Considers how cinema (and theatre) of the Blair era engages with the idea of Britishness during a time of devolution.
Dave, P. (2006) *Visions of England: Class and Culture in Contemporary Cinema*. Oxford and New York: Berg.
A detailed and illuminating study of the expression of class in popular and experimental British cinema.

Higson, A. (2003) *English Heritage, English Cinema: Costume Drama Since 1980*. Oxford: Oxford University Press.
A definitive analysis of recent costume drama from one of the most important scholars of British heritage cinema.

Korte, B. and C. Sternberg (2004) *Bidding for the Mainstream? Black and Asian British Film Since the 1990s*. Amsterdam: Rodopi.
Uses detailed case studies of black and Asian filmmaking from the 1990s and early 2000s to illustrate a shift towards the 'mainstream'.

Mather, N. (2006) *Tears of Laughter: Comedy-drama in 1990s British Cinema*. Manchester: Manchester University Press.
Mather's accessible study contextualises and evaluates some of the most well-known British films of the 1990s, emphasising the interaction between drama and comedy.

Murphy, R. (ed.) (2000) *British Cinema of the 90s*. London: British Film Institute.
This anthology gives a comprehensive overview of British film culture of the 1990s from a range of perspectives.

_____ (2006) *Directors in British and Irish Cinema: A Reference Companion*. London: British Film Institute.
Exhaustive guide to the work of British filmmakers past and present.

Pidduck, J. (2007) *Contemporary Costume Film: Space, Place and the Past*. London: British Film Institute.
This volume offers nuanced, theoretically informed readings of British costume drama.

Sargeant, A. (2005) *British Cinema: A Critical and Interpretive History*. London: British Film Institute.
An introductory, decade-by-decade synopsis of the development of British film culture.

Secondary Reading

Aitkenhead, D. (2007) 'Class rules', *Guardian*, 20 October. Available at: http://www.guardian.co.uk/britain/article/0,,2195645,00.html (accessed 1 January 2008).

Alexander, K. (2000) 'Black British Cinema in the 90s: Going Going Gone', in R. Murphy (ed.) *British Cinema of the 90s*. London: British Film Institute, 109–114.

Alibhai-Brown, Y. (2001) *Imagining the New Britain: Who Do We Think We Are?* London and New York: Routledge.

Allon, Y., D. Cullen and H. Patterson (eds) (2001) *Contemporary British and Irish Film Directors: A Wallflower Critical Guide.* London: Wallflower Press.

Anderson, B. (1991) *Imagined Communities: Reflections on the Origin and Spread of Nationalism*, revised edition. London and New York: Verso.

Ashby, J. and A. Higson (2000) 'Contemporary Cinema 1: Britain's Other Communities (Introduction)' in J. Ashby and A. Higson (eds) *British Cinema, Past and Present.* London and New York: Routledge, 247–8.

Baillieu, B. and J. Goodchild (2002) *The British Film Business.* Chichester: Wiley.

Barr, C. (1986) 'Introduction: Amnesia and Schizophrenia', in C. Barr (ed.) *All Our Yesterdays: 90 Years of British Cinema.* London: British Film Institute, 1–29.

Barton, R. (2004) *Irish National Cinema.* London and New York: Routledge.

Bourne, S. (2002) 'Secrets and Lies: Black Histories and British Historical Films', in C. Monk and A. Sargeant (eds) *British Historical Cinema.* London: Routledge, 47–65.

Brabazon, T. (2005) *From Revolution to Revelation: Generation X, Popular Memory and Cultural Studies.* Aldershot, Hants: Ashgate.

Bradshaw, P. (2007) '*28 Weeks Later*', *Guardian*, 11 May. Available at: http://film.guardian.co.uk/News_Story/Critic_Review/Guardian_review/0,,2076629,00.html (accessed 1 January 2008).

Brooks, R. (2007) 'Is it curtains for big British films?', *Times,* 21 October. Available at: http://entertainment.timesonline.co.uk/tol/arts_and_entertainment/film/article2689591.ece (accessed 1 January 2008).

Brown, G. (2000) 'Something for Everyone: British Film Culture in the 1990s', in R. Murphy (ed.) *British Cinema of the 90s.* London: British Film Institute, 27–36.

Brunsdon, C. (2000) 'Not Having It All: Women and Film in the 1990s', in R. Murphy (ed.) *British Cinema of the 90s.* London: British Film Institute, 167–77.

____ (2007) *London in Cinema.* London: British Film Institute.

Burnett, M. T. (ed.) (2006) *Screening Shakespeare in the Twenty-First Century.* Edinburgh: Edinburgh University Press.

Cartmell, D. and I. Q. Hunter (2001) 'Introduction: Retrovisions: Historical Makeovers in Film and Literature', in D. Cartmell, I. Q. Hunter and I. Whelehan (eds) *Retrovisions: Reinventing the Past in Film and Fiction*. London: Pluto, 1–7.

Chanan, M. (2004) 'The Independent Film Parliament 2003: A Report', *Journal of British Cinema and Television*, 1, 1, 108–11.

Chapman, J. (2005) *Past and Present: National Identity and the British Historical Film*. London: I. B. Tauris.

Chibnall, S. (2001) 'Travels in Ladland: The British Gangster Film Cycle, 1998–2001', in R. Murphy (ed.) *The British Cinema Book*, second edition. London: British Film Institute, 281–91.

Chibnall, S. and R. Murphy (eds) (1999) *British Crime Cinema*. London: Routledge.

Chibnall, S. and J. Petley (eds) (2001) *British Horror Cinema*. London: Routledge.

Cox, A. (2004) 'A Call to Arms: Alex Cox addresses the Film Parliament', *Journal of British Cinema and Television*, 1, 1, 112–19.

Dave, P. (2000) 'Representations of Capitalism, History and Nation in the Work of Patrick Keiller', in J. Ashby and A. Higson (eds) *British Cinema, Past and Present*. London and New York: Routledge, 339–52.

Davies, S. (2007) '*Heroes and Villains*', *Sight and Sound*, 17, 1, 64–5.

Donnelly, K. J. (2001) *Pop Music in British Cinema: A Chronicle*. London: British Film Institute.

____ (2007) *British Film Music and Film Musicals*. Basingstoke: Palgrave.

Egere-Cooper, M. (2006) 'Black new wave bites the bullet', *Independent*, 29 September. Available at: http://arts.independent.co.uk/film/features/article1769741.ece (accessed 1 January 2008).

Everett, W. (2005) 'Images on the Move: Reframing the Cinemas of Europe', *Screen*, 46, 1, 97–105.

Ezra, E. and T. Rowden (eds) (2006) *Transnational Cinema: The Film Reader*. London and New York: Routledge.

Farrell, K. (2003) 'Naked Nation: *The Full Monty*, Working-Class Masculinity and the British Image', *Men and Masculinities*, 6, 2, 119–35.

Fouz-Hernández, S (2003) 'School is Out: The British "Coming Out" Films of the 1990s', *New Cinemas: Journal of Contemporary Film*, 1, 3, 149–64.

Friedman, L. (ed.) (2006 [1993]) *Fires Were Started: British Cinema and Thatcherism*, second edition. London: Wallflower Press.

Gibson, P. C. (2000) 'Fewer Weddings and More Funerals: Changes in the Heritage Film', in R. Murphy (ed.) *British Cinema of the 90s*. London: British Film Institute, 115–24.

_____ (2003) 'Imaginary Landscapes, Jumbled Topographies: Cinematic London', in J. Kerr and A. Gibson (eds) *London from Punk to Blair*. London: Reaktion, 363–9.

_____ (2004) 'Otherness, Transgression and the Postcolonial Perspective: Patricia Rozema's *Mansfield Park*', in E. Voigts-Virchow (ed.) *Janespotting and Beyond: British Heritage Retrovisions since the Mid-1990s*. Tübingen: Gunter Narr, 51–64.

Gilbey, R. (2006) 'The death of arthouse', *New Statesman*, 20 February, 40–3.

Glover, J. (2007) 'Riven by class and no social mobility – Britain in 2007', *Guardian*, 20 October. Available at: http://www.guardian.co.uk/britain/article/0,,2195680,00.html (accessed 1 January 2008).

Griffiths, R. (2006) 'Introduction: Queer Britannia – a century of *sin*ema', in R. Griffiths (ed.) *British Queer Cinema*. London: Routledge, 1–20.

Hall, Sheldon (2001) 'The Wrong Sort of Cinema: Refashioning the Heritage Film Debate', in R. Murphy (ed.) *The British Cinema Book*, second edition. London: British Film Institute, 191–9.

Hall, Stuart (1998) 'A Rage in Harlesden', *Sight and Sound*, 8, 9, 24–6.

Hallam, J. (2000) 'Film, Class and National Identity: Re-imagining Communities in the Age of Devolution', in J. Ashby and A. Higson (eds) *British Cinema, Past and Present*. London and New York: Routledge, 261–73.

Hardy, M. O. (2004) 'Gendered trauma in Mike Leigh's *Vera Drake*', *Studies in European Cinema*, 3, 3, 211–21.

Hayward, S. (1996) *Key Concepts in Cinema Studies*. London: Routledge.

Higgins, C. (2007) 'New tax breaks see British film industry "firing on all cylinders"', *Guardian*, 24 July. Available at: http://www.guardian.co.uk/uk_news/story/0,,2133130,00.html (accessed 1 January 2008).

Higson, A. (1995) *Waving the Flag: Constructing a National Cinema in Britain*. Oxford: Clarendon Press.

Hill, J. (1999) *British Cinema in the 1980s: Issues and Themes*. Oxford: Clarendon Press.

____ (2000) 'Failure and Utopianism: Representations of the Working Class in British Cinema of the 1990s', in R. Murphy (ed.) *British Cinema of the 90s*. London: British Film Institute, 178–87.

____ (2001) 'Contemporary British Cinema: Industry, Policy, Identity', *Cineaste*, 26, 4, 30–3.

____ (2004) 'A Working-Class Hero is Something To Be: Changing Representations of Class and Masculinity in British Cinema', in P. Powrie, A. Davies and B. Babington (eds) *The Trouble with Men: Masculinities in European and Hollywood Cinema*. London: Wallflower Press, 100–109.

____ (2006) *Cinema and Northern Ireland: Film, Culture and Politics*. London: British Film Institute.

Hjort, M. and S. MacKenzie (eds) (2000) *Cinema and Nation*. London and New York: Routledge.

Hjort, M. and D. Petrie (eds) (2007) *The Cinema of Small Nations*. Edinburgh: Edinburgh University Press.

Ide, W. (2007) 'Outlaw', *Times*, 7 March. Available at: http://entertainment.timesonline.co.uk/tol/arts_and_entertainment/film/film_reviews/article1484254.ece (accessed 1 January 2008).

Jaafar, A. (2005) 'We gotta have it', *Sight and Sound* (*Black World Supplement*), 15, 7, 2–5.

James, N. (2001) 'They Think It's All Over: British Cinema's US Surrender', in R. Murphy (ed.) *The British Cinema Book*, second edition. London: British Film Institute, 301–9.

____ (2002) 'To be or not to be', *Sight and Sound*, 12, 1, 14–17.

____ (2007) 'Merging on the freeway', *Sight and Sound*, 17, 1, 3.

____ (2008) 'Dazzled and confused', *Sight and Sound*, 18, 1, 5.

Jays, D. (2005) '*Kinky Boots*', *Sight and Sound*, 15, 10, 74–6.

Johnson, B. (2006) 'How we laughed at these comic new regulations about films', *Telegraph*, 4 December. Available at: http://www.telegraph.co.uk/opinion/main.jhtml?xml=/opinion/2006/12/14/do1401.xml (accessed 1 January 2008).

Jones, G. (2006) 'Blair is most unpopular Labour PM', *Telegraph*, 11 May. Available at: http://www.telegraph.co.uk/news/main.jhtml?xml=/news/2006/05/10/nlab10.xml (accessed 1 January 2008).

Kaplan, N. (2004) 'The Death of the Working-class Hero', *New Formations*, 52, 94–110.

Karamath, J. (2007) 'Shooting black Britain', *Index on Censorship*, 36, 1, 142–7.

Kelly, R. (2000) *'Purely Belter'*, *Sight and Sound*, 10, 11, 60–1.

_____ (2001) *'Like Father'*, *Sight and Sound*, 11, 7, 44.

Kelly, R. T. (2004) *'My Summer of Love'*, *Sight and Sound*, 14, 11, 60.

Knight, S. (2002) 'The exploited', *Guardian*, 1 November. Available at: http://film.guardian.co.uk/features/featurepages/0,,823498,00.html (accessed 1 January 2008).

Kuhn, M. (2002) *One Hundred Films and a Funeral: Polygram Films, Birth, Betrothal, Betrayal, Burial*. London: Thorogood.

Lancioni, J. (2006) 'Cinderella Dances *Swan Lake*: Reading *Billy Elliot* as Fairy Tale', *Journal of Popular Culture*, 39, 5, 709–28.

Landesman, C. (2007) 'It's True – You Can't Buy Class', *Sunday Times: Culture*, 9 September, 10–11.

Lay, S. (2002) *British Social Realism: From Documentary to Brit Grit*. London: Wallflower Press.

Leach, J. (2004) *British Film*. Cambridge: Cambridge University Press.

Leese, P. (2006) *Britain Since 1945: Aspects of Identity*. London: Palgrave Macmillan.

Le Gendre, K. (2005) 'Don't Talk Black!', *Independent On Sunday*, 21 August. Available at: http://arts.independent.co.uk/film/features/article307052.ece (accessed 1 January 2008).

Leigh, D. (2000) 'Get Smarter', *Sight and Sound*, 10, 6, 22–5.

Leigh, J. (2002) *The Cinema of Ken Loach: Art in the Service of the People*. London: Wallflower Press.

Luckett, M. (2000) 'Image and Nation in 1990s British Cinema', in R. Murphy (ed.) *British Cinema of the 90s*. London: British Film Institute, 88–99.

Macallister, C. (2004) 'Contemporary British Cinema and the Re-imagining of World War Two: A Virtual/Humane Sensibility to War and a "New" Grammar of Heroism', in J. Irwin (ed.) *War and Virtual War: The Challenges to Communities*. Amsterdam and New York: Rodopi, 171–87.

Macnab, G. (2002) 'That shrinking feeling', *Sight and Sound*, 12, 10, 18–20.

_____ (2007a) 'Why the British have failed at Cannes', *Independent*, 27 April. Available at: http://arts.independent.co.uk/film/features/article2486990.ece (acessed 1 January 2008).

____ (2007b) 'British film: A new golden age?', *Independent*, 2 November. Available at: http://arts.independent.co.uk/film/features/article3119264.ece (accessed 1 January 2008).

Manovich, L. (2001) *The Language of New Media*. Cambridge, MA and London: The MIT Press.

Marris, P. (2001) 'Northern Realism: an Exhausted Tradition?', *Cineaste*, 26, 4, 47–50.

Mazierska, E. and L. Rascaroli (2002) *From Moscow to Madrid: Postmodern Cities, European Cinema*. London: I. B. Tauris.

McFarlane, B. (2001) 'The More Things Change ... British Cinema in the 90s', in R. Murphy (ed.) *The British Cinema Book*, second edition. London: British Film Institute, 273–80.

____ (ed.) (2003) *The Encyclopaedia of British Film*. London: Methuen and British Film Institute.

____ (ed.) (2005) *The Cinema of Britain and Ireland*. London: Wallflower Press.

McGill, H. (2006) 'Mean Streets', *Sight and Sound*, 16, 11, 26–8.

McKechnie, K. (2001) 'Mrs Brown's Mourning and Mr King's Madness: Royal Crisis on Screen', in D. Cartmell, I. Q. Hunter and I. Whelehan (eds) *Retrovisions: Reinventing the Past in Film and Fiction*. London: Pluto, 102–19.

____ (2002) 'Taking Liberties with the Monarch: The Royal Bio-pic in the 1990s', in C. Monk and A. Sargeant (eds) *British Historical Cinema*. London: Routledge, 217–36.

McLoone, M. (2000) *Irish Cinema: The Emergence of a Contemporary Cinema*. London: British Film Institute.

McRobbie, A. (2007) 'Postfeminism and Popular Culture: Bridget Jones and the new Gender Regime', in Y. Tasker and D. Negra (eds) *Interrogating Postfeminism: Gender and the Politics of Popular Culture*. Durham NC: Duke University Press, 27–39.

Monk, C. (1999) 'From Underworld to Underclass: Crime and British Cinema in the 1990s', in S. Chibnall and R. Murphy (eds) *British Crime Cinema*. London and New York: Routledge, 172–88.

____ (2000a) 'Men in the 90s', in R. Murphy (ed.) *British Cinema of the 90s*. London: British Film Institute, 145–55.

____ (2000b) 'Underbelly UK: The 1990s Underclass Film, Masculinity and the Ideologies of "New" Britain', in J. Ashby and A. Higson (eds)

British Cinema, Past and Present. London and New York: Routledge, 274–87.

____ (2002) 'The British Heritage-Film Debate Revisited', in C. Monk and A. Sargeant (eds) *British Historical Cinema.* London: Routledge, 176–98.

Mosley-Wood, R. (2004) '"Colonizin Englan in Reverse"', *Visual Culture in Britain*, 5, 1, 91–104.

Mottram, J. (2007) 'A clockwork outrage', *Times*, 8 March. Available at: http://entertainment.timesonline.co.uk/tol/arts_and_entertainment/film/article1483906.ece (accessed 1 January 2008).

Mullen, L. (2006) '*Red Road*', *Sight and Sound*, 16, 11, 78.

Mundy, J. (2007) *The British Musical Film.* Manchester: Manchester University Press.

Murphy, R. (1992) *Realism and Tinsel: Cinema and Society in Britain, 1939–1949.* London and New York: Routledge.

____ (2001) 'Citylife: Urban Fairy Tales in Late 90s British Cinema', in R. Murphy (ed.) *The British Cinema Book*, second edition. London: British Film Institute, 296–300.

Naficy, H. (2001) *An Accented Cinema: Exilic and Diasporic Filmmaking.* Princeton and Oxford: Princeton University Press.

Nowell-Smith, G. (2004) 'Reflections on the European-ness, or Otherwise, of British Cinema', *Journal of British Cinema and Television*, 1, 1, 51–60.

Nowlan, B. (2006) 'The Politics of Love in Three Recent US and UK Films of Young Gay Romance: A Symptomatic Reading of *Beautiful Thing, Get Real*, and *Edge of Seventeen*', *Journal of Homosexuality*, 50, 4, 141–84.

Ojumo, A. (2005) 'Loaded questions', *Observer*, 20 March. Available at: http://observer.guardian.co.uk/review/story/0,,1441507,00.html (accessed 1 January 2008).

O' Pray, M. (1996) 'The British Avant-Garde and Art Cinema from the 1970s to the 1990s', in A. Higson (ed.) *Dissolving Views: Key Writings on British Cinema.* London and New York: Cassell, 178–90.

Patterson, J. (2007) 'Why isn't this a British film?', *Guardian*, 7 September. Available at: http://arts.guardian.co.uk/filmandmusic/story/0,,2163376,00.html (accessed 1 January 2008).

Paxman, J. (1998) *The English: A Portrait of a People.* London: Michael Joseph.

Petley, J. (1986) 'The Lost Continent', in C. Barr (ed.) *All Our Yesterdays: 90 Years of British Cinema*. London: British Film Institute, 98–119.

Petrie, D. J. (2000) *Screening Scotland*. London: British Film Institute.

Pigeon, R. (2001) '"No Man's Elizabeth": The Virgin Queen in Recent Films', in D. Cartmell, I. Q. Hunter and I. Whelehan (eds) *Retrovisions: Reinventing the Past in Film and Fiction*. London: Pluto, 8–24.

Pirie, D. (1973) *A Heritage of Horror: the English Gothic Cinema, 1946–1972*. London: Gordon Fraser.

Rayns, T. (2006) '*The History Boys*', *Sight and Sound*, 16, 11, 58–9.

Rumbelow, H. (2007) 'The benefits for Britain of being Mr Bean', *Times*, 30 November, 21.

Sargeant, A. (2005) *British Cinema: A Critical and Interpretive History*. London: British Film Institute.

Shail, R. (2007) *British Film Directors: A Critical Guide*. Edinburgh: Edinburgh University Press.

Sinfield, A. (2006) 'Boys, Class and Gender: From Billy Caspar to *Billy Elliot*', *History Workshop Journal*, 62, 116–72.

Sinyard, N. and M. Williams (2002) '"Living in a World That Did Not Want Them": Michael Winterbottom and the Unpopular British Cinema', *Journal of Popular British Cinema*, 5, 114–22.

Smith, C. (2000) 'Travelling Light: New Art Cinema in the 90s', in R. Murphy (ed.) *British Cinema of the 90s*. London: British Film Institute, 145–55.

Spicer, A. (2004) 'The Reluctance to Commit: Hugh Grant and the New British Romantic Comedy', in P. Powrie, A. Davies and B. Babington (eds) *The Trouble with Men: Masculinities in European and Hollywood Cinema*. London: Wallflower Press, 77–89.

Stanley, R. (2001) 'Dying Light: An Obituary for the Great British Horror Movie', in S. Chibnall and J. Petley (eds) *British Horror Cinema*. London and New York: Routledge, 183–95.

Steyn, M. (1998) 'Two timing', *Spectator*, 2 May, 44.

Street, S. (1997) *British National Cinema*. London: Routledge.

____ (2005) 'The British Film Debate: Introduction', *Screen,* 46, 1, 85–6.

Thompson, D. (2004) 'Another England', *Sight and Sound*, 14, 10, 38.

Tookey, C. (1995) 'European Film Mountain', *Prospect*, 3. Available at http://www.prospect-magazine.co.uk/article_details.php?id=4940 (accessed 1 January 2008).

UK Film Council (2000) *Towards a Sustainable UK Film Industry*. Available at: http://www.ukfilmcouncil.org.uk/media/pdf/p/r/TASFI.pdf (accessed 1 January 2008).

Vincendeau, G. (ed.) (2001) *Film/Literature/Heritage*. London: British Film Institute.

Walker, A. (2004) *Icons in the Fire: The Rise and Fall of Practically Everyone in the British Film Industry 1984–2000*. London: Orion.

Watson, G. (2004) *The Cinema of Mike Leigh: A Sense of the Real*. London: Wallflower Press.

Watson, N. (2000) 'Hollywood UK', in R. Murphy (ed.) *British Cinema of the 90s*. London: British Film Institute, 80–7.

Wayne, M. (2006a) 'Working Title Mark II: A Critique of the Atlanticist Paradigm for British Cinema', *International Journal of Media and Cultural Politics*, 2, 1, 5–73.

____ (2006b) 'The Performing Northern Working Class in British Cinema: Cultural Representation and its Political Economy', *Quarterly Review of Film and Video*, 23, 4, 287–97.

Whitehead, T. (2007) *Mike Leigh (British Film Makers)*. Manchester and New York: Manchester University Press.

Wickham, P. (2003) *Producing the Goods? UK Film Production Since 1991: An Information Briefing*. London: British Film Institute National Library.

Williams, K. (2006) 'Keeping it unreal', *Guardian*, 29 September. Available at: http://arts.guardian.co.uk/filmandmusic/story/0,,1882771,00.html (1 January 2008).

Williams, L. R. (2005) 'The girl can't help it', *Sight and Sound*, 15, 4, 42–3.

Williams, M. (2006) '*9 Songs*', *Film Quarterly*, 59, 3, 59–63.

Wood, R. (1999) *The Wings of the Dove*. London: British Film Institute.

INDEX